THE PILGRIM

Essays on Religion

BY
T. R. GLOVER

FELLOW OF ST. JOHN'S COLLEGE, CAMBRIDGE, AND
PUBLIC ORATOR IN THE UNIVERSITY

*Author of "The Jesus of History," "Jesus in
The Experience of Men," etc.*

NEW YORK
GEORGE H. DORAN COMPANY

COPYRIGHT, 1922,
BY GEORGE H. DORAN COMPANY

PRINTED IN THE UNITED STATES OF AMERICA

R. G.

QUIDQUID EX ILLO AMAVIMUS
QUIDQUID MIRATI SUMUS
MANET MANSURUMQUE EST

PREFACE

A volume of collected papers must have some central idea, and perhaps that central idea is given clearly enough in the title and in the article that stands first. All the sections of the book turn upon the spiritual life, and on that interpretation of it which we find in the New Testament, in its precursors and in those who in art and life have developed and elucidated it.

The study of Jeremiah appeared in the *Expositor*. "The Meaning of Christmas Day" was written at the request of the Y.M.C.A. for distribution in the British Army, and it was reprinted, I understand, by the wish of the American Y.M.C.A. for the American Expeditionary Force. Two other papers in a somewhat different form were in a small booklet, once published by the Student Christian Movement under the title of *Vocation*, and now out of print. Others rest on contributions to the *Nation* and other journals, but have been completely rewritten. Four at any rate have not been in my writing before.

CONTENTS

CHAPTER		PAGE
I	THE PILGRIM	13
II	THE MAKING OF A PROPHET	22
III	AN ANCIENT HYMN OF HATE	40
IV	THE MEANING OF CHRISTMAS DAY	51
V	THE TRAINING AT NAZARETH	61
VI	THE TALENTS	84
VII	THE LAST EVENING	105
VIII	THE WRITER TO THE HEBREWS	119
IX	THE HOLY SPIRIT	143
X	THE STATUE OF THE GOOD SHEPHERD	174
XI	THE RELIGION OF MARTIN LUTHER	200
XII	A LOST ARTICLE OF FAITH	221
XIII	THE STUDY OF THE BIBLE	243

THE PILGRIM

THE PILGRIM

I

THE PILGRIM

The pilgrim seems to be dropping out of our religious conceptions. There are hymn-books which still keep a place for pilgrim hymns, but they are probably not often sung, except by children. And we are told often enough that the sentiment is false—if the hymn-writer insists that he is "but a stranger here," it is his own fault; earth is not, as he asserts, "a desert drear"; and the reference of all happiness to another world is unsound, and, perhaps, unchristian. On the contrary, R. L. Stevenson is a good deal nearer the mark:

> The world is so full of a number of things,
> I'm sure we should all be as happy as kings.

So he wrote in the "Child's Garden of Verse," and the couplet stood for a poem in itself. The greater part of his work is to the same tune—the world is a good place, planned to be so by "our cheerful General on high," and, indeed, achieved, if you will only have the sense "to be up and doing," and take the gladness of it. If you grumble:

> Bleak without and bare within,
> Such is the place that I live in,—

he bids you look better at it; why, if nothing else, the very frost of winter will "make the cart-ruts beautiful," and, in short,

> To make this earth our hermitage
> A cheerful and a changeful page,
> God's bright and intricate device
> Of days and seasons doth suffice.

So the pilgrim passes out of the picture with his medieval trappings, sandal shoon, and shell and staff. He is gone, and the excursionist has taken his place.

> I'm sure we should all be as happy as kings.

That the world is a good sort of place is not, after all, a very novel idea—it is in the first chapter of Genesis curiously enough, for in general it is credited with being Greek rather than Hebrew. The Greek, we all know, lived in the beauty and glory of the world, and, what is more, he interpreted it for all time. Take, for instance, Pindar's picture of the baby Iamos hidden among the flowers. The child of a god, he is a child of shame, some would say; but look at him, as he lies wrapped in a cloth under the flowers, and mark the lavish richness of the colours. It is the *ion,* in whose rays his tender body is steeped (the phrase is the poet's), that

THE PILGRIM

gives him his name. Where is the shame? A healthy child, half-god by birth, with a heroic story, a god-given inheritance, heaven lying about him in his infancy, and a house of heroes founded ere he dies. A beautiful world, and full of glory—who has limned it better than Pindar, or loved better the gleam of its life and colour? And yet at the end Pindar strikes another note.

τί δέ τις; τί δ' οὔ τις; σκιᾶς ὄναρ ἄνθρωπος.

"What are we? What not? Man is a shadow of a dream." Curious how Greek melancholy is bound up with Greek love of beauty! And the same thing meets us elsewhere. Spenser stands in English literature as the poet of "the worlde's faire workemanship," and the poet haunted with the thought that

Nothing is sure that grows on mortal ground;

for, when he weighs well the words of Mutabilitie, it causes him to loathe

This state of life so tickle,
And love of things so vain to cast away;
Whose flow'ring pride, so fading and so fickle,
Short Time shall soon cut down with his consuming sickle.

It seems that, if we are not exactly pilgrims, we are like the horses in the chariot-race at the theatre. We may not be progressing, but the stage slips away under our feet. In fact, as the Red Queen said to Alice, it takes a great deal of running to stay in the same place. If we are not very careful, we shall find ourselves strangers in the most familiar scenes —old faces gone and new come, old ways and words forsaken, and new habits and new language surging in. We are not pilgrims, but we live in a progression. The difference is that the pilgrim looks forward, and does it more and more eagerly, while we look back with growing wistfulness. "The world passes away," wrote the old writer; "love not the world." Or, if you love it, pray to die young, when the evil days come not, when you are not yet solitary, when men do not yet count you some queer relic of the past, a curiosity from an older time, and a time they count inferior to their own.

Now the pilgrims were ready for all this, for they were curiosities from the start. When they passed through this fine world and saw its houses, lands, trades, honours, preferments, titles, kingdoms, pleasures, and delights of all sort, they passed, as it seemed, through a lusty fair, with no mind to the merchandise, and without laying out so much as a farthing. And a great stir they made by this conduct; and, as their chronicles tell us, there were reasons for this. First, the pilgrims were clothed with such kind of raiment as was diverse from the raiment of any that traded in the fair. The people, therefore, made a great gazing upon them; some said they were fools, some they were bedlams, and some that they were outlandish men. Secondly, and as they wondered at their apparel, so they did likewise at their speech; for few could understand what they said; they naturally spoke the language of Canaan. Thirdly, the pilgrims set very light by all their wares, and when one chanced mockingly to say, "What will ye buy?" they, looking gravely upon him, answered, "We buy the truth." On examination, they owned they were pilgrims, and strangers in the world, and that they were going to their own country, which was the heavenly Jerusalem.

So wrote John Bunyan, with an old Greek writer's words at the back of his mind—"These all died in faith, not having received the promises, but having seen them afar off, and were persuaded of them, and embraced them, and confessed that they were strangers and pilgrims on the earth. For they that say such things declare plainly that they seek a country." That Greek writer, as plainly, had studied one yet older, who had spoken of a place above the heavens, of an ideal city there laid up, and of man as "no plant of earth but of heaven"—οὐράνιον φυτόν. And if Bunyan had read the "Faerie Queene," or even the first book of it, as Giant Despair and some other features might tempt us to think, his heavenly city has yet another link with Plato—that goodly City,

> That earthly tong
> Cannot describe, nor wit of man can tell;
> Too high a ditty for my simple song.
> The Citty of the greate King hight it well,
> Wherein eternall peace and happinesse doth dwell.

Anyone who will read the "Gorgias" will see how the men of this world called Socrates, and, no doubt, his wonderful pupil too, fools and bedlams, how they wondered at their speech (for few could understand them), and how strange men thought their passion for Truth. How odd that a man should call this life a practice for death, that he should speak of a glorious vision beyond sense, and urge that our preparation should be "seeking the Truth"—and this in Athens, with Aristophanes living in the next street, and Cleon and his successors, as practical Empire-builders as ever turned a nation away from virtue and mercy, and such fine words! Strange, too, that in that city, which stood unique in all Greece for the intensity of its culture, and its love of beauty, yes, which in itself was the actual "education of all Greece," men should "desire a better country, that is, an heavenly"!

The pilgrim, with his foreign air, the language of Canaan, and the strange gaze that will have Truth, above all with his conviction that there is a heavenly reality which is his home—he is an uncomfortable spectacle for us. God sends sometimes rain, and sometimes sunshine; let us be content to take fair weather along with us. We like that religion best that will stand with the security of God's good blessings unto us; for who can imagine, that is ruled by his reason, since God has bestowed upon us the good things of this life, but that He would have us keep them for His sake? And the pilgrim, the idealist, is for hazarding all at a clap. No, the world is not as bad as he thinks; our city will not be destroyed with fire from heaven; we have learnt better. Instead of forsaking his city, why not do something for it? There are many who would help. A Charity Organization Society would, at least, be something; Mr. Legality would gladly aid, and the pretty young man his son, Mr. Civility, would make the very ideal secretary. At all events, let us go quietly; let freedom slowly broaden down; let us mend things cautiously, or we may upset more than ever we can put right. But he says No; he will hazard all at a clap. He neither regards prince nor people, law nor custom, nor Sir Having Greedy, nor the rest of our nobility. And he means what he says, and goes armed—as strange a spectacle as Don Quixote—and his speech is the speech of a bedlam. His gaze is fixed on something far off, toward which he will go; but if you ask him what he sees, it seems the perspective glass shook in his hand, and he could not look steadily—he thinks he saw something like a gate, and some of the glory of the place—so that, if you roundly tell him there is no such place, the best he can say is that he has heard and believes there is; he does not know. This is indeed hazarding all at a clap. And yet—

And yet who ever cared for Truth, and was not a stranger in a strange land, a pilgrim through shams, delusions, vanities, and compromises—a bedlam in whom every child of convention could read absurdity writ large?

Who ever sought the good of his fellow-citizens, and did not pass, sooner or later, for a quack and an advertiser, or, at best, a dreamer who could only stammer that he thought he saw the gate, and some of the glory, and could not tell the way to it?

Who ever lived, as seeing the invisible, putting his faith in the existence of a God, hazarding all for Him, and never had to face mockery and shame, and the hideous doubt that, at the end of it all, the Great Perhaps might turn out to be nothing—*vacuam sedem et inania arcana?* The bitter folly of his quest, who knows like the pilgrim himself? He must own Religion in rags, as well as when in his silver slippers; and stand by him, too, when bound in irons, as well as when he walketh the streets with applause—in short, he will be made the off-scouring of all things; and the very sensitiveness of soul that has set him on this pilgrimage, leaves him doubly tender to pain, contempt and rejection, and to doubt and despair.

The pilgrim is not gone. The moods of sentimentalism, in their play upon lazy natures that will think nothing out, may have turned our fancies elsewhere; but whether we dream, in our idle way, of him or of something else, he is treading our streets the same as ever, clad in a garb of his own,

THE PILGRIM

the strange speech on his lips, his gaze strained afar, and yet curiously keen in seeing through what is near. The real, the eternal, the spiritual—there is an appeal in them that Vanity Fair does not understand, nor Mr. Worldly Wiseman and a great many more respectable citizens, nor again many of those Greeks of whom we talk so much, perhaps not Pindar himself at heart. But as Wordsworth tells us, "the immortal mind craves objects that endure"; and it was made for them and finds no rest till it rest among them with their Author and its own. No, the pilgrim is not gone; he is still seeking the Celestial City—that kingdom of Heaven which has cost the world so many good lives, the way to which is marked by a cross for every milestone, and which mankind will not have at any price, and yet knows in its heart it must have.

II

THE MAKING OF A PROPHET [1]

One of the most profitable studies is to know the man to whom a call to some high task has come, and to find out, if he lets us so far into his heart, how it came to him. Where the call of God is heard by a man with any measure of obedience, there can seldom be for long any great doubt as to the history of it. Sometimes he will tell it us himself, vividly and directly, as Isaiah tells how he "saw the Lord sitting on a throne, high and lifted up, and his train filled the temple" (Isaiah vi.). But that is not the whole story, for if we ask who was this man to whom this vision came, and why should he have had it rather than anyone else, we are involved in a good many questions. If we can find the answers to them, we shall be in a position better to understand how God deals with men—how, historically, He has dealt with men; and when we understand that, we may find that He has had dealings with us ourselves, the significance of which we did not see.

It is perhaps rather a risky thing to enter on such

[1] I have to thank Dr Theodore H. Robinson, Lecturer in Hebrew at University College, Cardiff, for reading this paper, and for his criticism.

THE MAKING OF A PROPHET

inquiries when one is dependent on translations and is not at home in the vernacular spoken by the man we study. But I begin to think that a foreign speech is never fully mastered, however long one reads it;—do we know our own? And again, when a thought reaches a certain elevation, it may lose something in translation—a great deal perhaps—and yet reveal a great soul in awful simplicity. "And His will is our peace"—that is, even in a foreign prose, a thought of power and wonder, and it speaks, for those who will hear, of a spiritual experience of no common kind. Without Italian, we shall not know Dante to the full; but we can know something worth while of the greater sort of man from even a very little of him. One of Shakespeare's most famous women speaks thirty lines only in the course of the play. So, if we recognize that we are to lose something, we may also fairly claim that we do not lose all; when we read so living a man as Jeremiah in translation.

He tells us a little about himself and his antecedents. He was "the son of Hilkiah, of the priests that were in Anathoth in the land of Benjamin" (i. 1), a member by birth of a priestly caste, which does not always imply much religion but which sometimes explains reaction against a priestly view of religion and of God. The episode of his purchase of land (ch. xxxii.) seems to suggest that he was a man of some means. He further tells us (xvi. 2) that he did not marry. The rest of his story must be gathered from the things of which he speaks and the way in which he speaks of them.

It has been remarked of our Lord and St. Paul, that it is plain from their speech that the one was country-bred and the other a man of municipalities—"a citizen of no mean city," he says himself. The same contrast would appear to hold between Jeremiah and Ezekiel. Similes from nature are frequent in all literature, but there are differences in the way in which men use them. Our Lord always confined himself to the real and the actual, and so does Jeremiah; and there is a certain likeness in their use of country things and country ways, though Jeremiah does not employ the parable-form with anything approaching the supremacy we find in the Gospels. But contrast him with Ezekiel. The eagle, with great wings and long pinions, full of feathers, which comes to Lebanon and carries off the topmost of the young twigs of a cedar and sets it in a city of merchants in a land of traffic (Ezek. xvii. 2-8),—the other cedar, under whose shadow "dwelt all nations" (Ezek. xxxi. 6),—and the lioness with the wonderful whelps (Ezek. xix. 1-9), leave nature a long way behind; and we are perhaps right in thinking that men who have lived close to nature take fewer liberties with her. Ezekiel draws his imagery less from nature than from Babylonian art. Jeremiah's references to country life, to the farm, the

THE MAKING OF A PROPHET

animals wild and tame, the daily round of labours and anxieties, and the wonder and beauty of nature, surely have something to tell us of a sentient spirit, for whom all these things were familiar and were dear. The examples of Virgil, and Wordsworth, and Tennyson, of Jesus himself, prompt the thought that Jeremiah's instinctive recurrence to country scenes and doings whenever he wishes an illustration that will reach the heart and make the matter clear and living, points to boyhood and its impressions.

It is wonderful how many sides of country life he touches—perhaps he would have been surprised to be told it himself. There is the vineyard, with the "noble vine, wholly a right seed," and "the degenerate plant of a strange vine" (ii. 21), and the grape-gatherer (vi. 9).[1] There is the olive; and here we may pause to note a certain deliberate use of the adjective, not idle at all, which suggests feeling and gives a hint of the man's style—"a green olive tree, fair with goodly fruit" (xi. 16)—and we may compare the question "where is the flock, that was given thee, thy beautiful flock?" (xiii. 20). There is the cornfield of course. "What is the straw to the wheat? saith the Lord" (xxiii. 28). That is not quite the Lord's dialect when He speaks with the city-bred. One of his most haunting phrases turns

[1] I omit other references in chapters xlix. to li., as the ascription of the chapters to Jeremiah is questioned, but they too contain interesting pictures—the vineyard (xlix. 9); the lion (xlix. 19, 20, li. 38); the scattered sheep (l. 17); the eagle (xlix. 16).

on harvest—"The harvest is past, the summer is ended, and we are not saved" (viii. 20). He thinks of a harvest much earlier than ours in a more genial latitude. After harvest the preparations begin for next year and new cattle are broken in—Ephraim, he says, is "chastised, as a calf unaccustomed to the yoke" (xxxi. 18).

As the boy grows, he ranges further afield—with the fowler after the birds—"they watch," he says of the wicked, "as fowlers lie in wait; they set a trap, they catch men" (v. 26). He studies the birds— "the stork in the heaven knoweth her appointed times; and the turtle and the swallow and the crane observe the time of their coming" (viii. 7); as to the partridge (xvii. 11) it is suggested that he depends here on a legend of the countryside, as White of Selborne followed the popular tale of the swallows lying congealed together under ponds in winter. Or perhaps he wandered with the shepherds— stretched the tent with them and set up the curtains (x. 20; vi. 3); and later on he looked back to the desert life and wished he could have it again (ix. 2). He told the flocks with them (xxxiii. 13), and grew into acquaintance with the wild beasts, notably the lion. The jackal, perhaps referred to in iv. 17 as the watcher of the fields, the leopard (xiii. 23) and the wild ass [1] (ii. 24) we can believe, had all

[1] The text appears doubtful. The Greek of the LXX. shows considerable variation.

THE MAKING OF A PROPHET 27

their interest, and the wildest and most dangerous of all the desert-dwellers no less—"by the ways hast thou sat for them, as an Arab in the wilderness" (iii. 2).

But apart from the living creatures,

> The earth
> And common face of Nature spoke to him
> Rememberable things.[1]

There is the great drought—"because of the ground which is chapt, for that no rain hath been in the land, the plowmen are ashamed, they cover their heads. Yea, the hind also in the field calveth and forsaketh her young, because there is no grass. And the wild asses stand on the bare heights, they pant for air like jackals; their eyes fail, because there is no herbage" (xiv. 4-6). That passage shows the man—the keen observation, the memory, the short, quick, telling phrase, and the picture, alive with truth and imagination. There is the "[hot] wind from the bare heights in the wilderness" (iv. 11), and in telling contrast we read: "Shall the snow of Lebanon fail from the rock of the field? or shall the cold waters that flow down from afar be dried up?" (xviii. 14). "Are there any among the vanities of the heathen that can cause rain? or can the heavens give showers? art not thou He, O Lord our God?" (xiv. 22). There is the constant and familiar mys-

[1] "Prelude," i. 586.

tery of day and night—"the shadows of the evening are stretched out" (vi. 4) and "the host of heaven that cannot be numbered" (xxxiii. 22) rise over the boy in the shepherds' camp, and the sense for God grows. Then back into the village to watch the potter busy at his wheel (xviii. 1-4), and the metal-worker (x. 4, 9) and the bellows blowing fiercely (vi. 29), the mud field-oven, familiar still in the East and elsewhere (i. 13). It is, in short, a boyhood like Wordsworth's in close touch with objects that endure.

From what has been said, it will take little insight to infer a meditative temperament. There is a reflective cast about him from the start, tinged with melancholy. He is given to introspection, and life with many moods lacks ease. Popular talk has exaggerated—grossly—his weeping and his tears, and the impression has been strengthened by the ascription to him of Lamentations. His contemporaries saw another Jeremiah—"a man of strife and a man of contention to the whole land" (xv. 10). He turns things over and over—"Thy words were found and I did eat them; and thy words were unto me a joy and the rejoicing of mine heart: for I am called by thy name, O Lord God of hosts. I sat not in the assembly of them that make merry, nor rejoiced. I sat alone because of thy hand; for thou hast filled me with indignation" (xv. 16, 17). He looks into his own heart—"pained at my very heart;

THE MAKING OF A PROPHET

my heart is disquieted within me" (iv. 19),—and, like other men who look within, he is shocked and troubled at what he finds, for "the heart is deceitful above all things, and it is desperately sick; who can know it?" and he answers, only God (xvii. 9). "O Lord, I know that the way of man is not in himself: it is not in man that walketh to direct his steps. O Lord, correct me" (x. 23, 24). As he grew to know better the life of his people—the hopelessness of effort to help or guide them—the inevitable doom descending on them, which he was to share—it is easy to understand how melancholy grew upon him (viii. 18; ix. 1), and how he wished he had never been born (xx. 14); but even before all this, the seeds of disquiet were with him.

A striking trait in his character is the extraordinary frankness with which, deeply pious as he is, he challenges God to explain Himself—"Righteous art thou, O Lord, when I plead with thee: yet I would reason the cause with thee; wherefore doth the way of the wicked prosper? wherefore are all they at ease that deal very treacherously?" (xii. 2). A similar question is asked by Theognis and other Greeks, but with them it is not a matter of religion. The Zeus to whom they address their inquiry is not the personal Jehovah of Jeremiah. The sensitive nature, coming gradually into the knowledge of the badness and rottenness of human character and human life, suffers acutely; the times are out of joint—there is so much to explain, and to endure; and the prophet (not yet at all conscious of any prophetic gifts or call) cannot explain and cannot bear, for he has not in himself the power to do either. Such a man, as he sees later on, is not the type needed for a prophet, yet God calls him, and we after the event see why. It is the sensitive nature, for which things are unendurable and unintelligible, that sees and reads the problem true. He, of all men, has the best chance to know, for he feels the irreconcilable elements that other men miss, and cannot rest with them in a peace that is no peace. Finally it has to be remembered that the clue which later Judaism found to unravel the mystery of pain and failure upon earth was not in Jeremiah's hand; he has no doctrine of personal immortality—a strange fact, when we realize the grasp he had of God and man as personalities.

This then is our man, but now we reach a place where there is a gap in our story. With this type it is never easy to know where and when they become conscious of God—even when they tell us. For God is with them, and as they go they have, in George Fox's phrase, "great openings." Things stand out in a new way—they see—and all before seems dim by comparison. This happens again and again. When further, as in the case of Jeremiah, we depend on a book notoriously confused and uncertain in text and order, as the Septuagint translation sufficiently shows, a book about the writing of which we can never pronounce definitely how much the prophet wrote or Baruch or others, we cannot get very far with a narative. But we find sooner or later a man with an unspeakable consciousness of God. "Am I a God at hand, saith the Lord, and not a God afar off. Can any hide in the secret places that I shall not see him? saith the Lord. Do not I fill heaven and earth? saith the Lord" (xxiii. 23, 24). God, near and far, and filling all things—it is the knowledge of all the mystics. How can there be other gods? And yet the prophet's people neither see nor feel. "Hath a nation changed their gods, which yet are no gods? but my people have changed their glory for that which doth not profit. Be astonished, O ye heavens, at this, and be horribly afraid, be ye very desolate, saith the Lord" (ii. 11, 12), for over these very heavens God's people have set another. "Seest thou not what they do in the cities of Judah and in the streets of Jerusalem? The children gather wood, and the fathers kindle the fire, and the women knead the dough, to make cakes to the queen of heaven" (vii. 17, 18). Thus from childhood the minds of his people were being steeped in falsity, and years after in Egypt the women said that so long as they had burnt incense to the queen of heaven they had "plenty of victuals, and were well, and saw no evil," and things had gone wrong since they left off (xliv. 18). There were other renunciations of God, too—"for according to the number of thy cities are thy gods, O Judah; and according to the number of the streets of Jerusalem have ye set up altars to the shameful thing, even altars to burn incense unto Baal" (xi. 13). Here we have the beginning of the call—in the dreadful contrast between God and No-gods, between the prophet's sense of God's nearness and wonder, and the people who turned their back to God, and not their face (ii. 27).

The prophet looked out on the world around; the vision of God does not dull the eyes of understanding. No, with keener gaze he looked and he saw other nations—armies and kings and great powers—danger ever nearer. But no one else saw it. Poor and great alike are under delusion; false to God, false to one another, delusion has come upon them. Their very confidence in God is false. Isaiah had foretold the safety of Jerusalem from Sennacherib; plenty of new Isaiahs foretold in the same strain her safety from Nebuchadnezzar. It was in vain; God's thoughts were other. "Amend your ways and your doings, and I will cause you to dwell in this place (*or,* I will dwell with you). Trust ye not in lying words, saying, The temple of the Lord, the temple of the Lord, the temple of the Lord are these" (vii. 3, 4). The temple had been saved before, this time it would not be. God asked righteousness, but

THE MAKING OF A PROPHET

they were satisfied without it. But the place is full of prophets of peace—saying, "I have dreamed, I have dreamed" (xxiii. 25); and "they have healed also the hurt of my people lightly, saying, Peace, peace; when there is no peace" (vi. 14; viii. 11). The "hurt" here is a breakage not to be healed by words. "The prophets prophesy falsely, and the priests bear rule by their means; and my people love to have it so; and what will ye do in the end thereof?" (v. 31). And God has heard what the prophets have said that prophesy lies in His name (xxiii, 25).

The call comes to a point. The situation grows intolerable—false peace, real danger, rejection of God, rejection by God, captivity—"and my people love to have it so!" Then Jeremiah hears God speaking, and speaking to him personally. It does not matter whether the conversation took a moment or six months—it came. "Before I formed thee in the belly I knew thee, and before thou camest out of the womb I sanctified thee; I have appointed thee a prophet unto the nations" (i. 5). This is indeed a dreadful outcome of the realization of God—this awful charge—to be a prophet—to quit field and quiet, to speak of God and His judgments to men who will not listen, when one is a man, sensitive, shrinking, and uneasy. God must have chosen the wrong man. "Then said I, Ah, Lord God! behold,

I cannot speak, for I am a child.[1] But the Lord said unto me, Say not, I am a child: for to whomsoever I shall send thee thou shalt go, and whatsoever I command thee thou shalt speak. Be not afraid of their faces: for I am with thee to deliver thee, saith the Lord. Then the Lord put forth His hand, and touched my mouth, and the Lord said unto me, Behold I have put my words in thy mouth. . . . Gird up thy loins, and arise and speak unto them all that I command thee: be not dismayed at their faces, lest I dismay thee in their sight. For, behold, I have made thee this day a defenced city, and an iron pillar, and brazen walls, against the kings of Judah, against the princes thereof, against the priests thereof, and against the people of the land. And they shall fight against thee; but they shall not prevail against thee; for I am with thee, saith the Lord, to deliver thee."

"Peace, peace," when there was no peace, was the message of the false prophet. Jeremiah's message was to be judgment, the destruction of temple and tower, captivity in a strange land and no speedy return. And when the false prophet promised a short exile, Jeremiah had to write and give his countrymen a strange message from God—to settle down, to marry and multiply, "and seek the peace of the city whither I have caused you to be carried

[1] By "child" he means that he has never had responsibility; he is not a person whose words will naturally carry weight.

THE MAKING OF A PROPHET

away captive, and pray unto the Lord for it; for in the peace thereof shall ye have peace" (xxix. 6, 7); for they were to be there seventy years. So far every word of God that He puts in Jeremiah's mouth is a word of terror and pain. No man would wish to speak them—least of all such a man. And yet he could not help it. That we learn from the burning utterance that follows the conflict with Pashhur (ch. xx.). Here we have to remember the contemporary belief that God would receive a man to his damnation. The very word used by Jeremiah is employed by Ezekiel (xiv. 9), "if the prophet be deceived and speaketh a word, I the Lord have deceived that prophet and I will stretch out my hand upon him and will destroy him," and in the story told to Ahab by Micaiah (2 Kings xxii. 19-23). Jeremiah has become charged with words from God, and finds, or thinks he finds, that God does not fulfil them. It is the most terrible mood that a sensitive nature can experience. "O Lord," cries the prophet (xx. 7) after his public exhibition in the stocks, "thou hast deceived me and I was deceived; thou are stronger than I, and hast prevailed; I am become a laughing-stock all the day, every one mocketh me. For as often as I speak, I cry out; I cry, Violence and spoil: because the word of the Lord is made a reproach unto me, and a derision, all the day. And if I say, I will not make mention of him, or speak any more in his name, then there is in mine heart as it were a burning fire, shut up in my bones, and I am weary with forbearing and I cannot contain." Such words need no comment—they are true of every prophet, every poet, every man to whom God speaks; there is nothing for it but to speak what is given, and at last the given word comes out almost of itself.

Even yet we have hardly got the whole of the call, but we have seen certain elements of it—the consciousness of God and the sense of the all-importance of the God-directed life—the contrast offered by the nation's indifference to God, their need of God and their danger—the summons to speak, coupled with reluctance and a deep feeling of unfitness,—the growing, burning inevitableness of obedience—and somehow the conviction that God, Who fills earth and heaven, Who picks His man before he is born, must go with His messenger. Pain there will be—endless conflict with the men of his nation, prophet and priest and king—contumely, stocks and dungeon—and, at last deportation—a long record of failure. The brazen wall and iron pillar, the man of strife and contention (as they called him), stout, dauntless and impenetrable—they little knew how he quivered and tingled and suffered. The promise was fulfilled to the letter that he should be like a "brazen wall"; whatever his inward moods, revealed to us in his writings, his countrymen saw in him a man of brass, neither to be intimidated nor cajoled.

THE MAKING OF A PROPHET 37

At last he has to tell Israel that not only is God entirely independent of them and their worship, but that God is utterly done with them: "I have sworn by my great name, saith the Lord, that my name shall no more be in the mouth of any man of Judah in all the land of Egypt, saying, As the Lord God liveth (*i.e.* God will no longer be the God they swear by; he will no longer be *their* God at all). Behold, I watch over them for evil and not for good. . . . They shall know whose word shall stand, mine or theirs" (xliv. 26, 27, 28). The message was a hard one—doubly hard when it had to be given against his own people, when it bore the look of disloyalty and bad patriotism—and he gave it at all costs.

But then because he is obedient and risks everything on God, he is given a still deeper insight into God's nature and God's ways. They have turned the back to God and not the face, though He has sent prophet after prophet, "rising up early and sending them" (vii. 13),—so God is to be frustrate of His purpose? Is He? "Then came the word of the Lord unto Jeremiah, saying, Behold I am the Lord, the God of all flesh; is there anything too hard for me?" (xxxii. 26, 27). God's message given through Jeremiah has failed,—not altogether, for there were some who listened and remembered and wrote down his words—but in the main it had failed, and God is beaten? It is early to say that. No, God is not likely to be beaten—hardly that. Then?

By and by the prophet, despised and rejected along with his God, penetrates farther into the secrets of God. God's love of Israel and God's rejection by Israel meet, as it were (in Bunyan's phrase), in his soul; and which will prove stronger? "The Lord appeared of old unto me, saying, Yea, I have loved thee with an everlasting love" (xxxi. 3). If God's love is on the same scale as His other attributes, it will be as eternal as God Himself; it will in the long run prevail over Israel, and will achieve its purpose. A new Israel, ransomed and redeemed from the hand of him that is stronger than he, shall come back from captivity, "and they shall come and sing in the height of Zion, and shall flow together unto the goodness of the Lord . . . and my people shall be satisfied with my goodness, saith the Lord" (xxxi. 11-14). But it will be a changed Israel, and the change will be an inward one. "Behold, the days come, saith the Lord, that I will make a new covenant with the house of Israel, and with the house of Judah. . . . I will put my law in their inward parts, and in their heart will I write it; and I will be their God, and they shall be my people; and they shall teach no more every man his neighbour and every man his brother, saying, Know the Lord [the sorry task of the prophet himself]: for they shall all know me from the least of them

THE MAKING OF A PROPHET

unto the greatest of them, saith the Lord; for I will forgive their iniquity, and their sin will I remember no more" (xxxi. 31-34). The insight here is amazing—hundreds of years later the infant Christian church saw the meaning of the passage and took it, and gave the name of "New Covenant" to the book that told the story of God in Christ reconciling the world to Himself. The instinct that seized the quotation was sound; but how came the thought to Jeremiah? Surely by obedience to God's call.

God has many ways of calling men; but when side by side a man grows conscious of the love of God in Christ, with all it means of freedom and peace, and of the darkness of the heathen world, given over to gods that are no gods, and all they involve of falsity, cruelty, and lust—or when, in short, he realizes the distance between the actual and the ideal in any sphere—is it not legitimate to suggest that in such a contrast there lies a call for him also, and that, if he obeys, he too will enter into new knowledge of the love of God and of God's purposes?

III

AN ANCIENT HYMN OF HATE

Sometimes one opens an old book and a leaf of writing will flutter out—a letter written perhaps a hundred years ago or more, a letter that tells of passionate feeling, and gives one a glimpse of some great moment in the life of a man or woman forgotten, whose very name may have perished. There is something moving in thus stepping into the experience of another, seeing the eye flash, the lip quiver for a moment, and then realizing that this intensity of suffering or joy was long ago—long ago, and yet living still—and the rest silence.

There is just such a document in the Book of Psalms. Look at this:

> By the waters of Babylon,
> There we sat down, yea, we wept,
> When we remembered Zion.
> Upon the willows in the midst thereof
> We hanged our harps.
> For there they that led us captive required of us songs,
> And they that wasted us required of us mirth, saying,
> Sing us one of the songs of Zion.
> How shall we sing the Lord's song
> In a strange land?
> If I forget thee, O Jerusalem,
> Let my right hand forget her cunning.

AN ANCIENT HYMN OF HATE 41

Let my tongue cleave to the roof of my mouth,
If I remember thee not;
If I prefer not Jerusalem
Above my chief joy.
Remember, O Lord, against the children of Edom
The day of Jerusalem;
Who said, Rase it, rase it,
Even to the foundation thereof.
O daughter of Babylon, that art to be destroyed,
Happy shall he be, that rewardeth thee
As thou hast served us,
Happy shall he be, that taketh and dasheth thy little ones
Against the rock.

There is hardly so vivid a bit in the Old Testament itself, full as it is with gleams from the life of man. Look at the story of this unknown writer. He has seen the Babylonian come in appalling strength and sweep conquering through Palestine, from Damascus down to Jerusalem. There followed a siege, and then the city was captured, and the Babylonians marched in and sacked Jerusalem. There was unbridled ruthlessness about these conquerors from the Euphrates, which went beyond what is usually conceded to modern armies. A number of the better families of the Jews were gathered to be transported to the other side of the world. The sickly were left to their fate; needless infants in arms were disposed of, the psalmist tells us how. That savage cry at the end of his Hymn of Hate is a revelation; it was his own child that he had seen so treated. With his friends and fellow-citizens he was marched northwards, following more or less the route of General

Allenby. There is no other way from Jerusalem to Babylon; those who have tramped northward through Syria will best understand what that march was like. At the point where the Euphrates most closely approaches the Mediterranean they crossed the desert and marched eternally down the banks of that great river. The journey was long and tedious, but the fatigue and the hardship had this advantage, they kept men from thinking. At last they reached the place where they were to live, where their graves and the graves of their children are found to this day—Nippur. The journey was over, and they were in a new land. People have spoken of the pathos of seeing the emigrants embark at Liverpool for a new world; but at least they embark in hope, and one who has seen it feels a greater pathos in their disembarkation as immigrants at Quebec or Ellis Island. The promised land does not flow with milk and honey on the landing-stage.

Arrived in Babylonia, and sitting by the riverside, there is talk among the prisoners and their guards, for even Babylonians were human, and as they sit the Babylonians sing songs of their own land. By and by in a friendly spirit someone asks the Hebrew captives if they, too, will not sing. One of the happiest stories of our late war, whether it is true or not, describes a sing-song in an English trench, and then an English soldier says, addressing two prisoners: "Our friends Hans and Fritz will now oblige

AN ANCIENT HYMN OF HATE

with the Hymn of Hate." The story does not say what Hans and Fritz did; but one of the greater and finer features of the war was surely this, that, once made prisoners, they were among friends; their country was not destroyed, there was no sacked Jerusalem away behind them, no murdered children; there was detention, and then a safe return for them.

But for the Jew in Babylonia everything was different. There was no Jerusalem, there was no home, there was no return, there was no child; the child lay with its head dashed upon the rock where the ruins of the home stood, and dogs and birds had picked its bones. Nor was this all. "How shall we sing the Lord's song," he asks, "in a strange land?" For, like many of the ancients, he seems to have held the view that gods, like kings and princes, had their frontiers, within which they might be omnipotent, but outside of which they had no power. David himself said to Saul: "If it be the children of men that have stirred thee up against me, cursed be they before Jehovah; for they have driven me out this day that I should have no share in the inheritance of Jehovah, saying, 'Go, serve other gods'" (1 Sam. xxvi. 19).

The Babylonian soldier thought that it would be interesting to hear a Hebrew melody, to enjoy for a moment the contrast of the strange tune, even if he did not understand the words. But he got no song. The whole nature of the poet rose up quivering with pain. He left the group by the waters of Babylon, he broke away from them, and out of the sorrow that surged through him he wrote a new song altogether, full of tears and memories, culminating in this crash of hatred—the one great authentic Hymn of Hate in the Bible. People speak of the cursing Psalms; there is none of them with the concentrated, definite, distilled intensity of this. And so far as we know anything of the poet, there is the end of the story. Who he was, we do not know; what became of him, we do not know. We only know that he had gone into exile, and that, whether his life was long or short, in exile he died. Was he among those to whom the prophet Jeremiah wrote the terrible letter from Jerusalem?

Thus saith the Lord of hosts, the God of Israel, unto all the captivity, whom I have caused to be carried away captive from Jerusalem unto Babylon: Build ye houses, and dwell in them; and plant gardens, and eat the fruit of them; take ye wives, and beget sons and daughters, and take wives for your sons, and give your daughters to husbands, that they may bear sons, and daughters, and multiply ye there, and be not diminished. And seek the peace of the city whither I have caused you to be carried away captive, and pray unto the Lord for it; for in the peace thereof shall ye have peace. For thus saith the Lord, After seventy years be accomplished for Babylon I will visit you, and perform my good word toward you, in causing you to return to this place. For I know the thoughts that I think toward you, saith the Lord, thoughts of peace and not of evil, to give you hope in your latter end (Jeremiah xxix.).

Think of the feelings with which he heard the letter. The exile was to be for seventy years. He

AN ANCIENT HYMN OF HATE

would never return. If any of his should return, it would be his grandchildren, the third generation; and he is to pray for the peace of Babylon! To pray for the peace of Babylon—and he is exulting in the hope that somehow, some day, she may be destroyed, and he has prayed for blessing on the man who will kill the babies of the Babylonians as the Babylonians killed his child. Pray for the peace of Babylon!

However, it came to the seventy years. There the exiles were, and there they had to stay. It was not till Cyrus conquered Babylon that the Jews were allowed to return. But it was not the same Israel that went into exile that returned to Jerusalem. It has been suggestively said that Israel went into exile a nation and returned a church. Unlike the Bourbons of the nineteenth century, Israel in exile learnt some things and forgot others. Whether it was accident or genius that made the order of the Psalms, it is significant to find in the 139th a measure of the distance that was really travelled in religious experience. "How shall we sing Jehovah's song in a strange land?" asks the earlier poet in exile. The question of the later poet (later by some centuries) is quite different:

> Whither shall I go from thy spirit?
> Or whither shall I flee from thy presence?
> If I ascend up into heaven, thou art there:
> If I make my bed in Sheol, behold, thou art there:
> If I take the wings of the morning,

> And dwell in the uttermost parts of the sea,
> Even there shall thy hand lead me,
> And thy right hand shall hold me.
> If I say, Surely the darkness shall overwhelm me,
> And the light about me shall be night;
> Even the darkness hideth not from thee,
> But the night shineth as the day;
> The darkness and the light are both alike to thee.

Israel had gone into the uttermost parts of the earth, and had found that even there Jehovah's hand had led him, Jehovah's right hand had held him. Israel had learned that there is no land outside the range of God, that God is near all the lands, and is in all the lands, that he was as near to Jehovah by the waters of Babylon, as by cool Siloam's shady rill, and the Lord's hand was not shortened. In Babylon itself Jehovah had searched him and known him. But the later poet goes further in thought than the wings of the morning can bear him; he goes beyond the uttermost parts of the sea; he realizes (strangest of all) that in the grave itself God will be waiting for him. To the Hebrew the world of the dead was a dim, sad, gloomy place, all but without light and life. The most vivid picture given of it is in Isaiah's forecast of the fallen King of Babylon:

> Hell from beneath is moved for thee to meet thee at thy coming: it stirreth up the dead for thee, even all the chief ones of the earth; it hath raised up from their thrones all the kings of the nations.
> All they shall answer and say unto thee, Art thou become weak as we? Art thou become like unto us? Thy pomp is brought down to hell, and the noise of thy viols: the worm is spread under thee, and worms cover thee.

AN ANCIENT HYMN OF HATE 47

How art thou fallen from heaven, O day star, son of the morning! How art thou cut down to the ground, which didst lay low the nations! And thou saidst in thine heart, I will ascend into heaven, I will exalt my throne above the stars of God; . . . I will ascend above the heights of the clouds: I will be like the Most High. Yet thou shalt be brought down to hell, to the uttermost parts of the pit.

They that see thee shall narrowly look upon thee, they shall consider thee, saying, Is this the man that made the earth to tremble, that did shake kingdoms, that made the world as a wilderness, and overthrew the cities thereof; that let not loose his prisoners to their home? (Isaiah xiv. 9–17).

It was long before Israel included in its faith a really definite conviction of personal immortality. The poet of the 139th Psalm is one of the forerunners of this belief. "If I make my bed in Sheol, in the world of the dead, behold Thou art there." What a glowing presentment of the range and power of God! Down among the dead men in the dimness of Sheol, he finds Jehovah who has searched him and known him, who knew him before he was born, and is with him still.

The documents at which we have been looking are all genuine expressions of human experience; every accent, every note, every line is written, as it were, in heart's blood; and we see what it has cost to travel the distance between the two poets. We look back and we ask: "What was the meaning of the agony and misery of the earlier poet?" and we get the answer in the quiet happy faith of the later poet. Was it worth while, that deluge of disaster, those seventy years of exile? What has mankind to say in answer? Could we forgo the gain that Israel made in those years of suffering and hope deferred? No! We feel that it has worked out aright, at any rate, so far as mankind is concerned; we owe something to this poet by the waters of Babylon. And we sum up our conclusion as our own poets have summed it up—"Knowledge by suffering entereth"—"Our sweetest songs are those that tell of saddest thought." So it is again and again in the history of man; tragedy and pain, and nothing to do but quietly work through them, and the issue is peace to those who come after the sufferers, for whom they do their suffering and their thinking. Once this is realized, men find a new value, a new reality in suffering. It ceases to be mockery when it becomes intelligible; and some of the deepest natures will not wish to forgo it, if their suffering will produce such results for those they love, for those who are to come after them.

But what of the earlier poet and his unlightened pain, his anguish in the darkness? He sees no solution, and his pain is the more for his seeing none. But the later poet makes it clear that even he was not outside the range and knowledge of God, for sooner or later, whether in the uttermost parts of the earth, or in the world of the dead itself, he would know the touch and the face of Jehovah, and learn the explanation and be satisfied.

AN ANCIENT HYMN OF HATE

"How shall we sing the Lord's song in a strange land?" The strange land may be the old familiar home made strange for ever by a vacant place, by the estrangement of those dear to us, or by the coming of new thoughts that raise questions and seem to leave no place for God. Most men and women sooner or later know this exile, have to live in this strange land.

Our two old Hebrew poems give us the clue to find our way in the strange land which it may fall to us to travel. "Pray for the peace of the land," and do the ordinary duties of life, build up the home, care for the children, make friends with the Babylonians themselves; the most commonplace duties come first, and in the doing of them comes the realization of the prophet's promises fulfilled. "I know the thoughts that I think towards you," saith the Lord, "thoughts of peace and not of evil, to give you hope in your latter end." "Ye shall seek me and find me, and when ye shall search for me with all your heart, I will be found of you, and I will turn your captivity" (Jeremiah xxix. 11, 13, 14).

Such is the story of the Old Testament, and the New Testament, as ever, gives it new value, and raises it to a higher point. It tells of one hanging on a cross, who cries in agony, "My God, my God, why hast Thou forsaken me?" and dies without an answer from heaven. The New Testament also shows us the conviction of thousands that God was never more in earnest, never nearer, than when His Son hung upon the cross. "My peace I leave with you, my peace I give unto you": so they tell us Jesus said, and they were speaking from their experience. In the cross men find peace with God, and that means peace with men. There are no more hymns of hate; there is instead a New Song, and, as a New Testament poet says, it is sung by men of all nations and kindreds and peoples and tongues; the burden of it is thanksgiving and the keynote is joy.

IV

THE MEANING OF CHRISTMAS DAY

Everybody knows what Christmas Day is. We know it so well that we do not think about it. But it often repays us to think about the things that we know best, and without embarking on Theology we may say that Christmas Day commemorates the birth of the most interesting man known to history.

If it is objected that we have no means of knowing when he really was born, we can admit that at once. It was not till the middle of the Fourth Century that December 25th was chosen for the commemoration of the birth of Jesus Christ. The day had its own associations; it was a Roman festival time when, for a few days, all slaves were free and their own masters. It was also over a large part of the world kept as "THE DAY OF THE UNCONQUERED SUN." There was a widespread worship of the Sun; and, after the shortest day of the year and the dark days round about it, the growth of the Sun's light is evident on December 25th, and the day was kept as the birthday of the Sun. Not a bad day after all on which to remember the birth of Jesus, a day associated with freedom, the day that celebrates the birth of light.

This man's birth has meant both freedom and light to mankind, and it is worth while to let our minds rest on what he has done, on what he has meant to men.

Jesus stands for the God-centred life. There never was anyone for whom God was so real, for whom God was so near, and this sense of his for God lies at the very heart of all that he has done in bringing men freedom and light. It was not that he did not know the darkness and the limitations of ordinary life. As we read his story we can see that his was no easy life. If he believed in God it was not for want of knowledge of hell. He lived in a land enslaved by foreigners; he was a carpenter, he was poor. One of the early Fathers of the Church reminded the Christian rich that the Lord Jesus brought no silver footbath from heaven. He had to work for a widowed mother, for little brothers and sisters; he knew the tragedy of the money being lost, and the joy when it was found. He knew how hard it is to keep children in food and clothes, how fast they wear their clothes out, and how the time comes when clothes can be patched no more. He lived in a little town which, like other little towns, had its stories of squalor and pain, of broken lives, of prodigal sons, of oppression and tyranny. We can see in his story that he knew our problems, that he

THE MEANING OF CHRISTMAS DAY 53

knew above all where they hurt. "He suffered," we read in the New Testament, and it tells us what he did suffer—conflict of mind, temptation, repudiation; betrayal. The story is summed up as agony. All these things he knew, the commonplace troubles of ordinary people, the soul-destroying tragedies that from time to time break down the best and most beautiful spirits. He knew life, and he had the intellectual habit of taking the incidents of life without an anæsthetic, the hero's way of facing what is to be borne with open eyes and unflinching.

This man brings home to us, both by his teaching and by the story of his life, the possibility of real contact with God, not in mere moments of exaltation, but in the steady, sober business of life, in its enjoyments, in its sorrows, and in the happiness which we take without noticing. For him the centre of everything is God. God is not for him a vague abstract noun; he never defines God as if God were a problem in philosophy. But he lives on the basis of God, in the presence of God; he accepts God as a child accepts the best sort of father; God is *there*, God is good, and kind, and fatherly, and a friend, and a lover, One Who shares all our interests, Who never excludes anything in our lives from His mind or from His heart. Children always know when their parents are really interested in their affairs; the dolls, the stamp collection, the little house among the bushes, the bow and arrow. The great thing that

Jesus gives us is this conviction that God is interested in us, down to the last details of everything that appeals to our own minds and natures, and that He is interested in us because He is fond of us. For example, if you have not thought about these things, track down through the Gospels the references of Jesus to God's interest in colours. Jesus speaks of God's interest in the lily, which, he says, for beauty beats "Solomon in all his glory." It is quite clear that colour, and movement, and form, all the things that make the life of nature, appealed to Jesus, and he saw that they all appeal to God. Other teachers had taught men to use the ingenuity of the universe as an argument for the existence of a Mind behind it. Jesus was touched by the beauty of living things, and he saw that their beauty means that God, like every other creative mind, loves beauty. In this way Jesus brings God near to us; God, Who really likes and enjoys flowers and sparrows, would probably like little children, and Jesus says that He does.

It is not only that Jesus sees what a delightful nature God really has, but he is able to translate it into life. His knowledge of God is not like our knowledge of some things which we use when we want them (if we ever use them at all), but it is translated into life with this result, that it gives life a new worth-while-ness. His own life, his own personality, guarantee his insight into God. What is more, is the power he has of winning people to his outlook, of launching them on the new kind of life that he lived, and (seeing we are using a metaphor from ships) of steering them when they are launched, and safeguarding them from all the submarine activities of the enemy of life. That he does this still, is the experience of Christians.

Let us look a little at what his coming has meant in human history. Nothing has been more effective in safeguarding the individual man and woman from wrong and oppression than the conviction that he, or she, was one for whom Christ died. If Christ died for the slave, then we must at least be kind to him, and one day we shall set him free. If Christ died for the prostitute, then we shall have to rethink the conduct of life, and our whole estimate of women. There can be no exploiting people for whom Christ died. (This, by the way, is the essence of sin, the exploitation of man and the using of God's gifts against God.) Historically, where men and women have believed that Christ died for the least important of us, there has been a new honour for men and women, a new love for them, and a growing resolve that everything shall be theirs which their Great Friend could wish them to have. In this way Jesus has been the best champion of the people. Jesus increases the significance of men for one another; "he possessed and he conveys the genius for appreciation." The definition of a gentleman as "one who does not put his feeling before others' rights, or his rights before their feelings" is exactly in the vein of Jesus. There may be those who see little in courtesy and good manners, but Jesus saw their inner meaning, and he taught and practised them. They are a recognition of the dignity of God's children. There was a charm about his love that he has been able to transmit to many of his followers. Charm is an unconscious thing, and it is never really acquired by practice, but Jesus taught his followers to forget themselves, and many of them have learnt the lesson, and catching his spirit have caught a great deal of his charm.

Jesus was the great discoverer of the family. We are so familiar with the text "Suffer little children to come unto me" that we forget that a new and original thing it was for a great man and a great teacher to say. He believed in family life; he never taught that all the best men and women should not marry, he held with their marrying; and biologists to-day emphasize the boundless spiritual and intellectual gain to society, when, at the Reformation, marriage was given the significance that Jesus saw it has in God's scheme of things. It is pointed out how much the world owes to the good men and women who have married and brought up children. This is part of the freedom that Jesus has given us, and this, too, must be linked with his consciousness of God.

The Sixteenth Century saw the New Testament

THE MEANING OF CHRISTMAS DAY 57

translated into English, the story of Jesus made available "for the boy that follows the plough"; and the Seventeenth Century saw a great revolution in England, a great achievement of freedom. The Eighteenth Century saw the great campaign of the Wesleys to win men for Jesus Christ; the Nineteenth Century saw England abolish the slave trade, humanize her own laws, emancipate woman, and give her mind as never before to the interests of little children, not only on her own island, but all over the world. Why is it that where Jesus becomes a living reality for men, they are more human than before, larger of soul and of sympathy?

For a long time before Jesus was born, men had been wrestling with the idea that even foreigners are human. Jesus himself is the great pledge that we all are of one blood, "barbarian, Scythian, bond and free," English, German, Indian and Chinese. There is a certain truth in nationalism, but Jesus made humanity a real thing in God. He must lay the foundations for any League of Nations that is to be real and to last.

For the individual, Jesus has done wonderful things. His very existence has historically been a stimulus to thought. We forget sometimes that thought is a primary Christian duty. We forget the freedom of mind of Jesus, and his perpetual insistence on our thinking. "The truth shall make you free," we read; but the truth is not found at random, in the streets. Jesus has committed us to finding out and incorporating in life all the truth there is in God, to capturing the whole of God, and making God in all His fulness our own. He has not only set men this task, but he helps them to achieve it. Very much the same can be said about art as about the other regions of thought and feeling. One function of art is the enjoyment and the interpretation of "God's real" in its whole complex of relations. Was there ever anyone who enjoyed God more than Jesus did, or shared his joy in God more successfully with other people, communicating his joy to men and women? Jesus was more than what we call original, he was originative; he had the creative mind. His parables are masterpieces in the use of language, so easy and so simple that one would not suppose there was any art in them. That is the very acme of art. Jesus gave to the individual an infinite value, and by doing so he opened new fields to art. Wherever the story of Jesus has ruled, with its freedom and with its breadth, men have loved art and music and laughter, and have enjoyed all the simple and wonderful things that God gives. Humour has been defined as the sense of contrast touched by love, the power of seeing the finite on the background of the infinite. "The real sense of humour breaks into flower when we have overcome the world." Yes, and who overcomes the world? Who has the real peace of mind that is essential to humour, but those whom Jesus

THE MEANING OF CHRISTMAS DAY 59

has made free of the whole world, by showing them that they are the children of God, and that the world is the home God has made for them, and by giving them the courage to see God and to enjoy Him?

Jesus has enlarged the capacity of men for God; he has made us feel that the Author of every aspect of life touches the human spirit at every point. He has made us free, to develop our characters to the utmost; we are to be perfect as God is perfect. That includes every kind of perfection, intellectual and artistic, as well as moral and spiritual. Jesus has made God intelligible to us. He has brought God into our business and bosom, and he has given us the sense and the appetite for God. He has made us at home in God, and above all he has given us the feeling that the great joy of life is to realize God in every fibre of one's being, and to explore God through all the infinite maze of wonder and of love in which He shows Himself. Jesus has lit up God for us, turned light upon Him, and shown us that the great power of which we are fraid is the best Friend we have. In ancient days, and in the heathen world to-day, the object of religion is to get away from God. Jesus has changed all that, and made the object of our religion to get into the heart of God. He has interpreted God to us, for he himself is the bond of kinship between us. He is the author of peace, the giver of a happy mind, and that is why, to this day, we keep Christmas. Christmas is the Children's Day; what better day is there for them to keep than the birthday of the Great Friend, who (as it were) discovered them, who liked them, and was fonder of them than any of the world's great teachers, and who taught us all to love children with a new tenderness, and a new interest that the world had never known before?

So the ancient Church perhaps did not make a bad choice, when it chose the day associated with freedom and light, with the rebirth of nature, on which to remember the coming of Jesus. We shall use the day to the best purpose if we set our minds to work to discover, this Christmas, some new features of the Jesus whom we commemorate, if we read the Gospels over again and find out for ourselves what Jesus was and what he is. It is not a day on which we are called to celebrate a dead Jesus, but one which speaks to us of life and calls us to come face to face with a Friend, who is waiting to talk with us, to help us, to set us free, and to give us the light we need to face the darkness round about us.

V

THE TRAINING AT NAZARETH

I

A man who is to make anything of life, who means to capture the truth of things, must be, so Plato tells us,[1] the "spectator of all time and all existence"—"ever longing after the whole of things in its entirety, divine and human." In a universe which has a real unity about it, half-views will not do. We have to practise ourselves to get out of the habit of the half and be resolute to live in the whole, the good, the beautiful. So Goethe taught; and Thomas Carlyle used to like to quote the German, and generally quoted it wrong, substituting for the beautiful the true.[2] Perhaps a philosopher would prefer Carlyle's version; but in the end the difference grows less and less.

Jesus has been described as a peasant, unlettered and untravelled. Without saying so much in so many words, a certain school of commentators and historians cannot get away from the notion that the marks of his date and place are indelibly upon

[1] "Republic," vi., p. 486 A.
[2] See page 102.

him. Other men of his environment had certain beliefs; phrase suggestive of them is found among his sayings; therefore we can reconstruct him on the lines of his contemporaries, and he proves to have been of no very unusual type, pious, moral and fervid, but hopelessly loyal to an outlook that no intelligent man can keep, cloudy with dreams of miracle, and at last quite out of touch with reality, as unlike Plato's ideal man as one can well imagine. He tried, they say, to force the hand of God at last, and involved himself in death as the result of a desperate and untenable conviction that God *must* bring him back on the clouds of heaven—which did not happen; he was thus the victim of vulgar hallucinations, a peasant who had lost his balance and all sense of reality.

It is curious that so great a change in human thought should have been inaugurated by such a person; that so often a revival of religion has been brought about by a return to one whose central conviction was wrecked on the facts of history; that again and again men have found the courage to face the rethinking of the universe, physical and spiritual, in the stimulus of a poor creature with a central delusion. History is hardly to be interpreted on the lines of such an airy paradox; for history is always rational; and a solution of historical problems, that depends on life and the universal proving irrational, cannot be true. Carlyle may be little read to-day,

THE TRAINING AT NAZARETH 63

but he was right on many things, where fashion ignores him—right in his doctrine of the Hero, right in his conviction that all religions that have really moved mankind have a truth at the heart of them; right in maintaining that man is everywhere the natural enemy of all lies. A Christ who, however holy (whatever that vague word means), however pious, however beautiful, in his sublime morality and his trust in God and so forth, was yet mentally so deficient as to miss what men quite inferior to him could see at a glance, who would not face the facts of God but imposed on God a fanciful character of his own—such a Christ will not serve. Carlyle's Mahomed (I will not pronounce on his exact relation to the Mahomeds of more modern Arabists) was incomparably a stronger figure than this cloudy enthusiast;—to say nothing of Socrates and even Zeno —for they at least were teachers who based themselves on fact and on the ascertainable laws of the universe. The Christ of the apocalyptic school is not Hero enough to carry a great movement; and, ingeniously reconstructed as he may be, some very obvious historical factors seem to be omitted.

A peasant, unlettered and untravelled—so was Robert Burns, and it is hardly necessary to read Matthew Arnold's stinging criticism of his provincialism, or Carlyle's kindlier description of the narrow cranny in which Burns grew (Carlyle himself too a peasant), to realize how local, how commonplace, and how desperately the unlovely child of vulgar surroundings Burns could be; and yet he was what all the world knows and loves:

> Deep in the general heart of men
> His power survives.

So does the power of the Galilæan; and on ordinary lines of sane criticism, it is reasonable to ask what that power was. Burns' greatness is compatible with his baseness. The power of Jesus is unintelligible in conjunction with the imbecility of mind attributed to him in some quarters; and as the one is proved through all history and the other a theory of a day, further inquiry is obviously proper. Matthew Arnold was far nearer the mark when he said that Jesus was above his reporters; *they* were often peasants, and they certainly were not strong in letters, as Paul found and bluntly stated. Even modern historians have at times, involuntarily, shown us how trivial a great man can look in the portrayal of an inadequate interpreter. Probably few of us are quite adequate to the task of drawing Jesus as he was.

In any case, an inquiry into the early training of Jesus may help us to a better understanding of his capacity for the ordinary business of testing and comparing the values of ideas. All over the world we find more or less religious natures the ready prey of the first extravagant notion that is put plausibly to them; they have no background and no criticism.

THE TRAINING AT NAZARETH

But there is something to be said for the view that the training of Jesus provided him with both. If the Gospels supply the materials for the eschatologist's interpretation, they offer the evidence on which we can rely for a more natural one, one nearer the conception of Jesus which rational men have generally held. It is a sound canon that the evangelists have to be judged by Jesus, rather than Jesus by the evangelists. And after all they did not do their work so badly! They drew a great figure, which has obscured their slips and has been readily interpretable for all simple and sincere enough to recognize greatness when they see it. If the eschatologists insist on the letter of the Gospels where it suits them, a similar insistence may be forgiven to those who criticize their inferences. "Hast thou appealed unto Cæsar? unto Cæsar shalt thou go!" And it may be added that the texts and passages, to which we refer, have this advantage; they deal with ordinary and commonplace matters which do not involve miracle or marvel, which are taken for granted and only casually mentioned, and which could not appeal to any writer as bearing on any theory of the world's end.

II

To begin, then, with historical Galilee—"Galilee of the Gentiles." The country was only added to the Jewish kingdom about 100 B. C. by the conquering arm of "Aristobulus the King of the Jews," as he would be known in the world of the foreigner—Judas the high priest, as he was in Jerusalem. The people, like that of Edom, was forced to embrace Judaism, and "Aristobulus was thus the creator of the Galilee which we know in our gospels—a region whose population is Jewish in belief and practice, but Gentile to a large degree in descent."[1] In accent (Mark xiv. 70) and in environment the people differed from the Jews of the South. Twenty miles from Nazareth was the great Mediterranean port where Rome poured her soldiers and officials on the land.[2] Westward, across the little lake, was a region of Greek cities, famous in the history of Hellenistic culture; did not Meleager himself come from Gadara?

Galilee did not lie out of the world, and the world, it must be remembered, was Greek. The constant struggle of Judaism, from Antiochus Epiphanes to Herod, was against Greek institutions and Greek ways—the Greek hat, the Greek wrestling-ground, the Greek theatre, the Greek temple, and Greek idolatry. The subtlest engine that could be turned against Hebrew idealism was Greek culture. The Greek language must have been heard everywhere; Greek names abound, and are found among

---

[1] Edwyn Bevan, "Jerusalem under the High Priests," p. 115; Josephus, "Ant." xiii. 11, 4; Sir G. A. Smith, "Hist. Geogr. of Holy Land," 414, says this conquest may have been in the previous reign.

[2] Sir G. A. Smith, "Hist. Geogr.," p. 35.

THE TRAINING AT NAZARETH 67

the twelve apostles themselves: Andrew, the brother of the Galilæan Simon Peter, bears witness in his name to the diffusion of Greek. Nor were the Jews and Galilæans stay-at-home people; and, once outside the Aramaic-speaking countries, Greek would be their universal speech, the language of commerce, the "pidgin English" of the day; more useful, at any rate as far as the Adriatic, than Latin, and the prevailing tongue of Alexandria, the greatest of all Jewish centres, the ancient New York.

That Jesus was bi-lingual, that he, like so many contemporaries, spoke both Aramaic and Greek, would be hard to refute. His reported conversation with Pilate is positive evidence, and all probability points the same way. No language difficulties are hinted at when he crosses the lake to Decapolis, or travels in the direction of Tyre. A bi-lingual man may be dull enough—dull as a polyglot waiter; but there is nothing in the Gospels to suggest that Jesus was dull; on any hypothesis, however humanistic, he had one of the clearest of minds (esthatology for the moment ignored); and an original intellect, reinforced with two spoken languages, will draw from them a great deal more than the polymath from many. At the same time there is no indication that he had any acquaintance with Greek literature. But genius has a great "gift of doing without."

From external sources we know of the energy and enthusiasm with which the Jews taught their children, or secured that others should teach them. The synagogue included a school and a schoolmaster. If it is asked in the Fourth Gospel: "How knoweth this man letters, having never learned?" (John vii. 15),[1] it may be pointed out that "letters" in Greek and English is ambiguous; a "man of letters" commonly has gone beyond the alphabet. Quite apart from such an episode as that where Jesus reads Isaiah aloud in the synagogue (Luke iv. 16), the Synoptic Gospels imply a close knowledge of the Old Testament. Jesus refers to reading as freely and naturally as any modern teacher would: "Have you not read?" he asks.[2] Add then to two spoken languages a familiarity with the Hebrew text of the Old Testament, and you have a very fair refutation of the charge that Jesus was "unlettered." As to his being "untravelled," he did not see Greece and Italy, but he lived in a polychrome world, full of Greeks and Romans, and men of many other nationalities, in full consciousness of the Roman Empire and its universality and not unaware (how could he not be aware?) of the Parthian power beyond the Euphrates (Acts ii. 9).

But all this discussion of languages and book-learning is very naïve after all. Heraclitus long ago had said that polymathy does not train the mind, or certain other philosophers, whom he names, would

[1] *Cf.* Acts iv. 13.
[2] Mark xii. 26; Matt. xii. 3, 5; Matt. xix. 4; Matt. xxi. 42; passages referring to different incidents.

THE TRAINING AT NAZARETH

have stood on a higher level.[1] What did Jesus learn from what he read and saw and heard?

First, we can set down that freedom from the local and contemporary to which an intelligent knowledge of the history of one's own race and of other races will always prompt. In the Bible, as he had it, as he learnt it intimately and familiarly, Jesus was brought into touch with "all time" so far as the Eastern world knew it. Of course the history of the world was larger than that of the Jews. But the Jews in their day had contact with all the great races of antiquity, and a bright Jewish boy who knew and visualized the history of his own people was in possession of background and atmosphere. That he both knew and visualized it, let "Solomon in all his glory" bear witness—it was Jesus' own phrase and it tells of the inward eye—and David helping himself in the hour of need to the shewbread, Elijah with the Tyrian widow, the much-travelled Queen, and Naaman; and three of our instances are foreigners of three different races. So he does not quite lack the emancipating touch of History.

But the Old Testament stood for much more; it represented the sum of God's dealings with Israel, and of these he laid hold in no ordinary way. It is remarked that he preferred the prophets and psalmists. One scholar, at least, suggests that his favour-

[1] Heraclitus fr. 16 (Bywater).

ite was Isaiah [1]; but he was not a man of one book, and a good case might be made for Hosea or Jeremiah.[2] He has achieved, as his Jewish contemporaries did not, nor his Christian followers, at once an intimacy with the prophetic mind and an independence of it. He does not quote as the literalists do; he seizes the heart of the message or of the man. "There is an affinity of spiritual truth between the Old Testament passage cited and the use of it in Jesus' teaching. The spiritual significance is always there."[3] He propounds no theory of inspiration. It might be assumed that he simply accepted the current view, but his treatment of Moses and of the laws of the Pentateuch makes this unlikely. A teacher who quotes what Moses said, and follows it up clause by clause with the words: "But I say unto you"; who condemns Moses' opportunism on the question of divorce, can hardly be credited with the dull theories of automatic inspiration which other men held and still hold. He expresses his own experiences in Old Testament language (Mark iv. 12, vii. 6). Even in the hour of death on the cross the psalm comes to his lips (Mark xv. 34). Prophet and psalmist spoke to his soul from their own souls; he recognized the truth and power of what they said; his experience repeated theirs if it transcended

[1] Arno Neumann, "Jesus," p. 44 (Eng. tr.).
[2] Oscar Holtzmann, "Life of Jesus," p. 92 (Eng. tr.).
[3] Charles S. Macfarland, "Jesus and the Prophets," p. 107; cf. pp. 193, 196.

it; and their phrase gave him again and again the word he wanted.

On one who grew up in the word of prophet and psalmist, to whom God, the God of prophet and psalmist, was all, what impression would books of the apocalyptic type make? How many of them did he actually know? What evidence have we that they had anything like the diffusion or acceptance of the Scriptures? If it is urged that he borrowed from them his conception of the Messiah, it may be conceded that the Messiah is mentioned in some but not in all these books; but once again we must guard against supposing that genius can borrow an idea from the mediocre without transforming it. If he borrowed the name, a very little reading will show how he changed the content. But the apocalyptic Messiah was a dim and changeable figure, varying with the writer. The picture of the Suffering Servant in Isaiah is far more congenial to Jesus. A simpler illustration will be found in his picture of the Last Judgment, where the framework is more or less that of common acceptance, and every principle and nuance of the story is his own. If a man's central ideas are any index to his mind, and if the ideas are of more importance than the form in which they may be conveyed, then it is clear how little is the essential debt of Jesus to apocalytic literature. It is trivial, discursive, tribal, dull in imagination, and poor in spiritual value.

At the same time it should be remembered that the writers of the apocalyptic books were children of an age of difficult problems and widening outlooks. It is not established whether they taught their contemporaries, or merely learnt with them, to enlarge their conception of God to include all history, past and future; but that the habit of so conceiving of God was not unfamiliar is proved both by their books and by the New Testament. If Jesus read or knew any of the apocalyptic books, any influence they could have upon him would, taken in conjunction with that of the prophets and psalmists, be in the direction of emancipation and range of mind. But still it is hard to suppose that he depends on such poor books for what is his outstanding characteristic. All time and all existence—real history and real insight into the spiritual—these he found in the prophets; and trained in such a school, he had little difficulty in appraising the value of ideas, in books or out of them.

From another point of view, it is significant to realize what he thought of the Old Testament. It cannot have been altogether easy for him to acquire his intimate knowledge of it. The rolls were read in the synagogue; children were taught a good deal by heart; private reading of the books was possible only for those who had access to them. Would a carpenter's family have a set of them? Many questions rise here; the cost of the reproduction of the books must have been great; a carpenter's wages or earnings cannot have been big; a family of boys and girls to feed and clothe and train does not, in common experience, increase the margin for books. It is conceivable that for private and personal reading he had to have recourse to the synagogue copies—in the leisure of a working carpenter, when the books might be available, and when daylight served. That the family was one of quiet piety is proved by their habit of going to the synagogue, by their general surprise when Jesus preached there, by their affectionate dread of his new publicity, by his use of domestic phrase and illustration for the inmost things of the kingdom of God. The home training would be based on knowledge and love of the Old Testament; but his special devotion to its reading was a matter of personal work and sacrifice, achieved at a cost. And, whatever we make of him, a spiritual genius of his dimensions found it a vital part of his religious life to read and re-read the Old Testament. It is a significant fact. Matthew Arnold once defined culture briefly as a knowledge of the best that has been said; it is his variant on the phrase of Plato with which we began. The individual supplements his experience and corrects his deductions from it by the experience and the thoughts of the best men who have gone before him. One feels that if prophet and psalmist had something to contribute to Jesus and his development, we may not have realized how much more they have for us, nor what we lose by our slight assimilation of both the Testaments.

III

"As his custom was," says St. Luke (iv. 16), "he went into the synagogue on the sabbath day." The Sabbath was perhaps kept with more strictness in Galilee and the north than in Jerusalem and the south. What it meant to Jews can be seen in the fanciful but suggestive sayings of the rabbis. The obervance of the Sabath makes a man a partner of God in the creation of the world; by hallowing it Israel brings redemption to the world and bears testimony to the divine ordering of the universe.[1] But perhaps even better may one gather the historical significance of the Sabbath from the half-flippant and yet serious poem of Heine, "The Princess Sabbath," in which he describes how every Friday at sundown the fairy princess comes and transforms the dog to a man with a spiritual history, for twenty-four hours.

Mr. Abrahams tells us that the New Testament accounts of the preaching in the synagogues are the most precise we possess, that they refer to the normal and not to the exceptional, and that we may rely on them completely.[2] The books of the Maccabees show clearly that there was public reading from the

[1] See Israel Abrahams, "Studies in Pharisaism and the Gospels," pp. 131; 129.
[2] *Ibid.*, p. 7.

THE TRAINING AT NAZARETH

scroll of the law (1 Mac. i. 57, iii. 48), gatherings for prayer (iii. 44), and above all for the singing of hymns with such refrains as "His mercy is good, and endureth for ever."[1] This procedure, as the New Testament, Pliny's letters, and Justin Martyr's account show, as well as some passages of Tertullian, was taken over very naturally by the Christian church, and maintained till the end of the second century—with modifications required by the rites of baptism and the Lord's Supper, and perhaps the agapæ.

That it was Jesus' custom to go to the synagogue is confirmed by a number of similar episodes which follow the one that Luke records; but it is interesting to have the habits of Jesus noted for us as such. It is suggestive too. Here in the synagogue he found reinforcement; once again he was given the opportunity "to survey all time and all existence." Israel's law and Israel's history, in Pentateuch, prophet and hymn, are brought forward again in a manner hallowed by long association and by the knowledge that, all over the world, within and without the Roman Empire, wherever twelve Jews resided, a similar worship, rich with the same reminiscences, was being celebrated in the same simple and natural way. It was a step toward the fulfilment of Jeremiah's prophecy of the New Covenant (Jeremiah xxxi. 31).

[1] *Ibid.*, p. 2.

Israel and his history, the long quest of God, the great revelation, the Law of God—the public worship was indeed a survey of all time and all existence.

It was more. One cannot imagine that the synagogue services in Nazareth—a town, it would appear, little esteemed—would be anything but dull. Read the glowing account that Apuleius gives in his "Golden Ass" of the sacraments and ceremonies and pageants of Isis, and of her mysteries, with the vision of "gods of the world above, gods of the world below," and ask what he would have said to this little group of laymen and women, whose worship is listening to passages written in a book, reciting prayers and singing psalms—with the minimum of the music, the suggestion, the mystery, the exotic that he loved; plain sense and no sacrament. It must have been dull enough; and the addresses by "scribes" may have been rather heavy and too full of references to books; "the learned are not light-handed," as a French critic has said. Yet Jesus evidently found something in it; his imagination went deeper than Apuleius would have gone. If the sacred books gave him insight into the past, the people showed him the present. He must have known them all, and their family histories and characters; and in the synagogue he learnt, like Wordsworth, to see

> Into the depth of human souls,
> Souls that appear to have no depth at all
> To careless eyes.[1]

He had in a degree beyond us "among least things an undersense of greatest."[2] Here he saw them *sub specie æternitatis;* he looked before and after, realized the great traditions embodied in these lowly people, their part in handing them on and shaping the future (a lesson that may be remembered when we think of his extraordinary faith in his disciples), and above all God's interest in them all.

At a time when "organized Christianity" comes in for much censure, when hymn and prayer and sermon are found dull, it may be something to recall once more that for a mind of the build of Jesus there was contribution in sharing a much formalized worship with quite dull people. It may not be a triumph of the imagination to find dull what he found full of appeal, full of the call of God—least of all when it is his story that is read and sung and interpreted. Judaism was held together by the synagogue; Christianity too has always been maintained by the assembly of common people for a joint purpose, which no imaginative mind, no soul with a sense of history, can call dull—the association of men and women with a great past, a great future and an eternal God. If imagination fails us, there

---

[1] Wordsworth, xiii, 166.
[2] Wordsworth, "Prelude," vii, 734.

is a loyalty, a desire to know the experience of the Master, which must prompt to a deeper sense of the value of what at present fatigues us.

But to return to the synagogue and his habit of going there, an intimate knowledge of common people and God's ordinary ways is a corrective to wild hopes and cloudy dreams. A soul full of the knowledge of God, and how God has borne Himself in crisis of Israel and agony of prophet, will go deeper into things than the restless and hurrying Apocalyptist, will be less disposed to expect quick solutions of age-long processes, will have a deeper faith in God than to challenge Him to hurry and display.

IV

One last habit of Jesus remains—his practice of leisurely prayer on the hillside in the darkness. Leisurely—not that the hours or minutes were vacant, but there was no rush of hurry about it. "I will hear what God the Lord will speak," said the Psalmist (lxxxv. 8); and the rate at which one will hear what God says will not always be the same. I have tried elsewhere to write of Jesus' intercourse with God;[1] it lies beyond us; but till we fathom it and experience it, we shall not understand Jesus. But when one compares the conception of God, involved in what the eschatological school attribute

[1] "The Jesus of History," pp. 110 ff.

THE TRAINING AT NAZARETH 79

to Jesus, with the picture of God which he actually gives us, and set it in the light of the long nights of prayer, of intercourse with God, which the records preserve for us, the contrast makes the apocalyptic Jesus still less possible. He has surveyed all time and all existence at leisure with God, gone deep into God's purposes for mankind and for himself; and the outlook, the shallowness, the fever, attributed to him do not fit the man whom the gospels present to us. The whole character must be rethought.

V

The relations of Jesus with John the Baptist are not very clear in the New Testament. We have definite statements, but they do not tell us all that we could wish to know; and no ingenuity can fill the gaps in our knowledge. After baptism, Jesus turns to the desert for forty days, we are told. If we say in modern speech, that the carpenter leaves home and work, and spends six weeks in spiritual concentration, we may have some fresh glimpse of what happened. At the end of it, Luke tells us, that Jesus returned in the power of the Spirit into Galilee, that he taught in all the synagogues, and, preceded by a great reputation, at last came to Nazareth (Luke iv. 16).

There is some doubt as to the time of this visit, for Mark appears to put it later, and some scholars say bluntly that Luke deliberately moved it forward to a point earlier than the ministry in Capernaum. It is, however, arguable that it belongs at the beginning. Mary, it is observed, records that there was a sermon in the synagogue, but he gives no account of its contents (Mark vi. 1-6). It is assumed as "very likely" that Jesus himself chose the lesson in Isaiah "which he would certainly understand in a Messianic sense"; and it is conceded that Luke may have taken the episode from a good tradition.[1] But two comments may be made. First of all, the sermon is still lacking; even its gist is not given, and the text survives, hanging almost loose, one might say; while what follows hardly suggests that the discourse took a Messianic turn. If Mark is right in dividing clearly between his teaching before and after the confession at Cæsarea Philippi, one would not expect an abrupt announcement in the Nazareth synagogue. In the next place, Mr. Israel Abrahams presents a good case for the view that Jesus did *not* choose the passage he read.[2]

The prophet Isaiah, says Mr. Abrahams, was handed to Jesus; it was not his own selection, it was put into his hands. The word "found" does not mean that he looked for the passage, but that he "found" it ready, when he opened the manuscript, a roll and not a book, which, when he was done with it, he "rolled up" and gave to the attendant. The

[1] O. Holtzmann, "Life of Jesus," pp. 276, 277.
[2] See "Studies in Pharisaism and the Gospels," pp. 7-8.

THE TRAINING AT NAZARETH 81

manuscript, being a roll, was unrolled as required, and as column after column was read it was rolled up again from the other end. Jesus then appears to have taken it into his hands, one rolled-up part in each hand, and as he drew them apart, he "opened" at the place already selected and found the passage of Isaiah ready for him to read. If the text is not given in Luke exactly as it is in the Septuagint or the Hebrew, that is of little significance. The right to "skip" while reading the prophets is well attested. The passage then was very like what is called a *sors Biblica;* you open the Bible at random, or it may be Virgil, and the passage you light on is an oracle. It is said that King Charles I tried this with Virgil in the Bodleian, and hit on verses, only too prophetic for him in the fourth "Æneid." [1]

Let us see what would follow from Mr. Abrahams' explanation, if St. Luke's order of events holds. Jesus, after weeks of hard thinking in the solitude of the waste lands, comes to Galilee and begins to preach. He comes to Nazareth, the home-town, always the most difficult place, the centre of the least sympathetic criticism; if he had previously stood up to read in the synagogue, it would appear, from the general surprise at "his words of charm," that his neighbours had never heard him expound before. He stands up to read, a roll is put into

[1] So Mr T. E. Page, in his Commentary on "Æneid," iv. 615-620.

his hands; he draws the rolled-up ends apart; it proves to be Isaiah; and there before his eyes, unsought, are the crucial words, his very commission: "The spirit of the Lord is upon me, because he hath anointed me to preach the gospel to the poor; he hath sent me to heal the broken-hearted, to preach deliverance to the captives, and recovering of sight to the blind, to set at liberty them that are bruised, to preach the acceptable year of the Lord." A coincidence—or a message from God, a confirmation of all that has come to him in the wilderness? For a coincidence to coincide, we must remember, a previous correspondence is needed; if such thoughts were not in his mind, the passage might have been silent to him. It looks as if it spoke to him, as if (whatever became of the sermon and the audience) the text were associated with one of those psychological experiences which men recall as landmarks. Accident—you say; the man may let you call it what you like; what happened at that moment to soul and mind was decisive in his life. It is significant that, when the messengers of John come to Jesus (which Luke puts *after* this reading in the synagogue), and ask for a message, Jesus substantially quotes this passage; and there are other echoes of its phrases in his speech on other occasions.

But, if we are building too much on the Lucan order, none the less the fact stands that this passage of Isaiah is associated in Jesus' mind with his

THE TRAINING AT NAZARETH

call, with his Messiahship, to use the word which Peter employed. His call is linked with the words of a spiritual hero of his race of old time; one to whom in instinct and insight he stood very close; his call has upon it the stamp of the highest and truest experience of his people. If apocalyptic books contributed, directly or indirectly, in his own reading or in other men's quotations, to him, their gifts are controlled by the prophetic view of life and of God; the prophetic is not swamped in the apocalyptic. Further, the call shapes itself in words that describe the very people with whom he had worked and worshipped—the sad, the desolate, the broken, the poor, and poorer than they guessed themselves, that day in Nazareth. The past and the present are linked in the call, and both with God; "the spirit of the Lord is upon me." The great discipline of Bible, synagogue and prayer, "the survey of all time and all existence," has borne its supreme fruit.

VI

THE TALENTS

One of the things which, as the Gospels record, astonished Jesus was the slowness of men's minds, their want of insight, the dulness of their imagination. The Gospel of Mark gives instances of the disciples themselves shocking him by want of faith and want of intelligence. "To you it is given to know the mysteries," he said; and they did not know them; they ought to see, but they only half saw, only half realized, and constantly missed the point of what he was telling them. Not to pursue the subject over too wide a field, we may turn to a parable in which he sketches the danger of the slack or dull imagination.

I

It comes like a page of contemporary history. It would take some research in Tacitus and the other historians to say how often, since Rome had begun to interfere in the East down to the days when she was mistress of it to the Euphrates, members of royal and noble houses in the Eastern Mediterranean area went to Rome to secure thrones and kingdoms.

THE TALENTS

Herod, so-called the Great, was plunged into danger after the death of Julius Cæsar; he concealed his family with great difficulty in a rock-stronghold on the border of Judæa, and then went off in search of Mark Antony, or some recognizable constituted Roman authority, to regain his Jewish kingdom. Permission was readily given him, and he returned with the royal title, but, as if he were a mere pretender, he had to recapture his kingdom from the patriots. He did it at last, by means of Samaritan and Edomite troops and other mercenaries, and with the support of Roman legionaries. Once he had recaptured Jerusalem, his capital, his executioners made havoc among the noble families there. So in substance says Mommsen.[1] Again when Antony fell, Herod had to see Augustus and get his kingdom confirmed anew. He took the precaution of first killing the last male descendant of the Maccabæan house, then went to Rhodes and saw the Emperor, who extended and consolidated the kingdom. Augustus had his own opinion of Herod; he would feel safer, he said, as Herod's pig (ὖs) than as his son (υἱός). But Herod was a drastic and, on the whole, a capable man, and it was good policy to disturb as little as possible what gave promise of effective settlement. This was twenty or thirty years before the birth of Christ (31 B. C.). Herod lived

[1] Mommsen, "The Provinces of the Roman Empire," Vol. II. ch. xi. pp. 178 ff.

to 4 B.C. "There is probably," says Mommsen, "no royal house of any age, in which bloody feuds raged in an equal degree between parents and children, between husbands and wives, and between brothers and sisters." Yet Herod was an energetic and intelligent ruler; he built the Temple at Jerusalem to please the Jews,[1] the circus to please other people, imperial temples in Jewish towns to flatter Augustus; he made friends in the lands around, rebuilt Cæsarea, put down brigandage and defended his frontiers against the Arabs of the desert. But he died at last, and his kingdom was divided among his three sons.

Archelaus got Judæa, but he had to go to Rome to have the grant confirmed; and a Jewish embassy also went to prevent it, and to secure autonomy.[2] They plead their cases before Augustus in the temple of Apollo, and Augustus gave a part of Herod's kingdom to Archelaus as ethnarch. He was a thoroughly bad ruler, and Judæa in 6 A.D. was made a province of the second rank. In 37 A.D. Agrippa, a grandson of Herod and of the beautiful Mariamne, "about the most worthless and abandoned of the numerous Oriental princes' sons living in Rome," and the friend of the new Emperor Gaius, was rewarded with Judæa. Others of the family held tetrarchies or kingdoms at periods throughout the

[1] It did not please them; see Bevan, "Jerusalem under the High Priests," p. 157.
[2] Josephus, "Bell. Jud.," ii. 6, 1, 156; "Antiq. Jud.," xvii. 11, 1, 860.

THE TALENTS

century, and after the fall of Jerusalem Agrippa II. (to whom Paul spoke) kept a small principality till he died in Trajan's reign (about 100 A.D.).[1] Probably the Herods were not the only noble family occupied with getting and losing kingdoms at the hands of the Romans in the Orient, whose adventures might be told among the Jews.

It is not at all unlikely that Jesus knew the story of Archelaus, and everybody knew the dynasty. So that this parable, at any rate, was drawn from more or less contemporary history, and no names were needed. The whole thing is full of actual life. It is noticeable that there are other parables, or fragments of parables, which turn on a somewhat similar theme—the absent master and the slaves in charge; and in at least one of them are traits taken, it would seem, from the old story of Ahikar. The traduced and vanished uncle reappears, suddenly vindicated, and the wicked nephew bursts asunder in surprise and remorse. But we need not linger over them, nor perhaps lay too much stress on Archelaus. The ruler, pictured by Jesus, shows more of the first Herod, we might say. The historical background is ample and certain enough; but Jesus tells the story for his own purposes, he handles it freely, and gives no names. The situation, the men in charge, and the developments that follow the King's return are the main points.

[1] Mommsen, "Provinces," ii. p. 219.

II

The nobleman of the parable sets off for Rome, and leaves his servants in control of everything. He had no one else to leave. Even Roman Emperors down to Claudius had in general no others on whom to depend than freedmen and slaves. As soon as possible the nobleman's fellow-citizens, who hated him, sent their embassy with all speed. The short sketch of Josephus leaves us room to surmise what went on in Rome—what networks were woven of intrigue and counter-intrigue, what bribery there was of Imperial freedmen and chamberlains and secretaries, and of everybody who could be supposed to have access to them or influence over them. In Archelaus' case all Rome's ghetto got to work. It meant endless money; and it serves in part to explain the interest attaching to the procedure of the servants in charge in the East, whether slaves or freedmen.

We need not pursue these Roman manœuvres, but they affect our story in that the uncertainty of the issue was felt in the home-land every day. It was "even chances" whether the nobleman or the embassy bribed the right man or caught the Emperor at the right moment; for we are not tied down to Augustus, and in the reign of Tiberius everything was more chancey. It was possible, too, that the nobleman would never come back at all; there were risks of sea and land; or the Emperor might detain him in Rome and banish him. Anything might

THE TALENTS

happen, and no man could foresee the event. The servants were living in a definitely hostile atmosphere; every patriot in the country was ready to do them an ill turn if they were loyal to their master, and eager to abet them in any disloyalty. To detach them from Herod's cause would help the country's; to neutralize them with courtesies, or bribes, or other seductions, was patriotic. And all the time there was the chance that, in the language of statesmen, they were putting their money on the wrong horse. The combination of uncertain success and steady ill-will was enough to unsettle many men.

Some of the servants perhaps reflected like the man in the other story (Luke xii. 45): "My Lord delayeth his coming," and took like him to beating the men and women slaves under him, to eating and drinking and being drunken; and at last were surprised by the triumphant return and the horrible doom suggested in that parable. But the wasters and their fate are not very interesting either to us or to the teller of the tale.

The servants who put their mind on their work are lightly sketched in the original, but there is no harm in lingering over them and trying to recapture what lineaments we may. Here is one of them, a quiet sort of man who says very little, who listens casually to what men say, who drifts around markets and seems to do very little; he sits about with men doing business or talking over business done. You do not catch him in any hurry or fussing about work; is he doing anything? After a while, if you watch, you notice that, though he seems constantly to have leisure, he frequents a particular type of society—not wasters, but men who occasionally drop information, which he hardly appears to notice—detail about crops and their prospects, odd facts about markets and freights, the movement of goods, rumours of the outside world, caravans turning up from the further Orient, chances a man might use if he cared to pick up stuff from Persia or India—not much in it perhaps, but it might turn out all right—movements of troops and random tales of where they are to be marched or quartered; all sorts of casual talk, not very unlike what you may hear to-day from men at loose ends for the moment, chatting of what may while away the time, talk of little account, but yet with information in it. So the stream of conversation ripples on; and then it turns out that this easy-going listener has caught a gleam or two among the pebbles, so to speak,—has guessed at alluvial gold being a possibility—has acted. These men would have lied if they had thought there was anything he specially wanted to know; they would have been alert at once, if they had guessed how much interested he was; but he showed no sign. Only those who got on his trail found that he had used the chance remarks about crops, had compared and sifted them with unsuspected shrewdness, had cornered grain quickly, and despatched it by muleteers returning empty to where the troops were to be stationed; he had picked up odd things from the caravans, listlessly bargaining or making friends with the Persians; he always knew what prices were, though he said little about them and never asked and never noticed very much, and he had a pretty shrewd idea what they were going to be. He kept turning his master's money over, oftener than men realized, though they came by and by to gather that he was doing pretty well, and began to attend to him, to give him information with one motive or another. In fact, he that hath, to him shall be given and he shall have abundance (Matt. xiii. 12); after a while he always knew what he wanted to know, picked it up, or got it out of the man who knew, and would help him in return—making friends with mammon, even if it had a little taint here or there of unrighteousness (Luke xvi. 9).

Another was of a different type, a good deal blunter and more direct. Someone whispered to him of a scheme that was to undo Herod, of the extraordinary advantages for him in it, how well worth his while he would find it; what did he think of it? And he said abruptly that he didn't think of it; and there was an end of it. He was a marked man after that; all Herod's enemies watched him, some eager to trip him, some glad to keep out of his way. He hammered along at his task, got work and plenty of it out of his underlings, made his lands do their work, an acre with him had to do an acre's job; and he would have no slacking in man or beast or field. He was up early and to bed late, and saw to things himself; he worked harder than the first man appeared to do, and made less of it. But his blunt loyalty had done good; men knew where he stood, and he was a great strength to people who were a little uncertain.

III

At last the news came that the Emperor had made up his mind. Augustus in his old age had not always been very quick or clear about details of foreign policy; and Tiberius (the reigning Emperor) more and more resented making decisions, he liked to leave things ambiguous, and to postpone questions; drift settled his policy very often. However, our story tells us that the unnamed nobleman got the award he wanted and came back to be king. The whole situation was acutely changed; there was no longer the least uncertainty about the future, and the prospective king's character was fairly known. The waster and the drunkard began to try to pull things together, of course unsuccessfully. The second of the two men we studied said in his abrupt way, with a grunt of satisfaction: "I knew he would pull it off," and drove on with his work. The first man said, as usual, very little, but seemed rather more

THE TALENTS

occupied than before; he had more now to do than any of them; his money was everywhere, and there was a lot of it, and he had to get it in—a little grieved, here and there, that one or two more likely coups must be let go now; but his affairs were endless in their ramifications, and he must have all ready for an audit—which, however, did not seem to worry him. So Herod came home.

How the kingdom had been governed we need not inquire closely. The new king would take it over and manage it, as the Roman government had, and the previous king, as the Seleucid emperors before him had, and Alexander before them, and the Persians before Alexander. Little change was wanted or necessary; in the Orient the old ways go on and a wise ruler can "make do with them," provided that the men at the crucial points are reliable. The system never changes very much. The census twenty years ago in Syria was taken much as under the Roman emperors, and one man, whom I heard telling of it, narrated how he had orders to go to Beyrout to be enrolled as he "belonged" there—the same arrangement that St. Luke records (ii. 1-4), and that we find in the papyri.[1] The vital point was the selec-

[1] *Cf.* G. Milligan, "Greek Papyri," No. 28. Gaius Vibius Maximus, Prefect of Egypt (says): "Seeing that the time has come for the house to house census, it is necessary to compel those who for any cause whatsoever are residing out of their nomes (*nomoi*) to return to their homes (*ephestia*), that they may both carry out the regular order of the census, and may also attend diligently to the cultivation of their allotments." This order belongs to the year A.D. 104.

tion of the right men for the key-positions. This is the explanation of the abrupt delegation of faithful servants to the charge of cities, roughly answering to the talents they had accumulated. There is also a play in the Semitic language on the words used for talents and cities—there are exactly the same letters in each, but in a different order.

Herod is now absolute master of the country, kingdom or tetrarchy or whatever it is; and he proposes to govern it on the old lines and make of it all he can. He has to keep the people quiet, without revolts or scandals that could reach Rome—the precaution which Archelaus neglected. But, if there are no public disorders or scandals, he has a free hand, and he proposes to squeeze out of his subjects the utmost possible. It is not a lofty idea of monarchy, but many great houses have held it or something very like it, down to King Leopold II in our own day. All over the territory things will have to be looked into—especially the personnel; and he must have at the top men whom he can absolutely trust—as viziers, if the word is not too large for them. It has never been so important for him to be absolutely sure of the character of his men; they may have their faults and vices, but he must be able to rely on their loyalty, their energy and their intelligence. They must be the men to see instantly what is to be done, to foresee and to forestall what hostile persons or groups will do, to leave nothing to chance, and to recognize an indication when they see it, and, whatever is to be done, to do it first, before anybody else can get started. It is with this object primarily that he holds his inquiry. No doubt he is interested in seeing how his affairs stand; but the contemptuous way, in which he hands over the restored talent to the servant who made ten, is proof that money was not now his chief interest; he wanted men.

The drunkard and the wastrel are not long in reaching outer darkness—weeping and gnashing of teeth. Herod's career has given him opportunity to read character, and that type is quickly read. Then follow the two men we have described.

The one has ten talents to show. No one would have guessed he had done so well. Herod takes a quick, sharp second look at him; "He'll do!" he says to himself; and the man gets "Well done!" It is to be noted that if Herod recognized his man, his man knew him before; he had seen in him, no doubt, the qualities later enumerated, and had not misliked them; frankly, he had admired Herod, and "Well done!" from Herod's lips would set him recalling the *laudari a laudato viro,* if he knew so much Latin. All sorts of people may praise you, and it is mere fulsome vanity; but let the master-hand take notice of your work! you do not want words, if you catch him interested. So much for the man, and we can understand the upwelling of pleasure in him, even if the quiet face familiar to us betrays only a shade more feeling than usual. But let us try to understand Herod too—the relief and satisfaction with which he hails the discovery of quality in this man and in the sturdy loyalist of the square jaw, who brings him five talents. They are men who have worked steadily and faithfully when his fortunes were at the darkest, who have the wit to watch and venture and achieve, men sturdily and successfully identified with their master, who had believed in him before his fortunes were established. If his praise was swift and lavish, it was meant, as his instant proposal of a great new opportunity shows; he believes in them and can reward their faithfulness in very little, as he now puts it, by making them rulers over much, by giving them at once work on a large and more splendid scale and reward out of all proportion to what they have done.[1]

IV

But the servant with one talent is the man on whom Jesus has spent most care in this story, drawing him with an individuality which he did not elaborate in the two faithful men. That they have character, is implied by the whole narrative; but as Jesus groups his picture at last, they stand for the moment, as it were, one on the right hand and the

[1] Luke xix. 17, 19; Matt. xxv. 21, 23; *cf.* also Luke xii. 44; the point is not accidental.

THE TALENTS

other on the left of their master, figures worth our attention indeed—but the centre is held by the new king and this curiously-drawn servant of his. It is as if Jesus meant us to study him with closer interest. The man is not exactly a bad servant; he would be classed by most of us in quite a different category from the drunken and wasteful slave of the other parable—but Herod has a different opinion, he groups them. The man has a sense of responsibility; and he certainly has an eye for character. He makes it quite clear that he understands the Herod type— he sketches it to the life—and the conclusion of the story shows in the king's words and acts, in his treatment of this man himself, and of the plotters who sent the embassy to Rome, but the delineation was so far right. But the man had never realized what his knowledge meant. He knew the value of property, and he took care of it in the traditional way of the Orient. On the day that I left Madura in Southern India in 1915, a little pocketful of Roman gold pieces of the first century, coins of Nero and Domitian, in excellent condition, were dug up in the compound of a factory. The man was not to be blamed, surely, for doing what the cannier members of every family had always done and do still. Probably hundreds of the sovereigns that have disappeared from our use are under ground in India and Arabia, hundreds and thousands. The man did not like the incessant speculation of the first servant;

it was risky. He does not see that use implies risk, and that money and other endowments are for use; he takes care of them, and misses the fact that his safe line of keeping the treasure absolutely intact and secure against loss means simply the depreciation of the treasure with the very loss he is guarding against. He is a hoarder, a matter-of-fact person, very commonplace in spite of his shrewdness; and he gives himself away. He does not understand currency, or opportunity.

He does not understand his master. How he expected his master to tolerate his plain language, we can only guess; perhaps Herod would have taken it from the second servant, with a laugh. But if this man draws Herod's character aright, how could he expect him to be satisfied without the interest that his wealth should bring him? But he fails in another way, and more hopelessly. As a critic of his master, shrewd as he is, he fails (as shrewd critics do) by getting the harder and meaner features of the king, and missing the large and generous traits in his character—the capacity for giving warm and glowing praise—the keen appreciation of character and energy, that marks the man of action. He knows the hard, exacting and cruel Herod; he misses the Herod of expanding ideas, the Herod of the new monarchy. He had never really understood the hopes and the passion of his master, he had never quite believed in the kingdom to be, he had not seen

THE TALENT

the future with its possibilities, he had been content to safeguard the present and let the future go. He had no imagination, no sense of a situation, no vision. And now—of what conceivable use is he? He has shown he cannot be trusted with the work most urgent to be done—what sort of use could he be with his prudential half-views, his reluctance to face facts and act on them, his half-knowledge of men, his inability to commit himself to any action that implies faith either in the future or in his master—and his consummate self-satisfaction? The swift and incisive Herod is done with him—has him hurled contemptuously out—and turns headlong to his next business, which, as we have seen, happens to be that blending of policy and violence that makes so large a part of Oriental king-craft—action and insight (of a kind) once more in this man of force. The cool brutality of the house shocked the Romans; to us it may suggest once more how absurdly out of place this man would have been in Herod's service.

V

Elsewhere Jesus spoke of men who seeing see not, and hearing hear not, and never understand. Here he has drawn a picture of the type; why did he think it important to draw him with such care? Or are we to throw the emphasis elsewhere, with some critics, and think chiefly of the lord who goes away and returns within a measurable time? Is Jesus necessarily thinking of a speedy return, on the clouds, that literalist obsession which some scholars insist on sharing with him? Why is it that when two readings, two interpretations, are possible, some will always have us take that which definitely lacks genius? Did Shakespeare mean to write of the dying Falstaff, "his nose was as sharp as a pen, on a table of green fields" (or baize), or do we owe that to two blunderers, who did not understand the famous knight, nor know his story, nor guess that the dying man, who "cried out God, God, God, three or four times," "babbled o' green fields"? Must the dullest reading, the most lack-lustre meaning, always be right? Shakespeare was not matter-of-fact. Jesus was greater than his commentators; there was more life, and fuller, in him; and there is really more danger of under-interpreting his words than of finding too much in them, at any rate, for those of us who are not his equals. We need not limit his meaning here to a speedy second advent, nor his moral to the platitude "let every one seek to increase his religious possessions."[1] There is a spaciousness, a width of range, in all his talk; it is apt to cover a good deal of life. There are all sorts of talents; and, if Jesus does not claim that "the natural gifts of his disciples were derived from himself," he probably

[1] I take this interpretation from the pages of a great scholar.

THE TALENTS

would not, if questioned, exclude them from the consideration of those whom his parable reaches.

The drift of the parable, for those who have ears to hear, and take the trouble to hear, should be clear enough, even if he did not unfold it, allowing some interpretations and excluding others. There are talents entrusted to a man, by God, by Jesus, perhaps by other men—natural capacity, charm, vision of the real gospel, learning, responsibility or even money. Does he realize the seriousness and the potentialities of the gift, the urgency of getting to work with it for the absent Master of all gifts, the amazing return that such work can yield in immediate result, in praise from above, in magnified opportunity? Take the parable in conjunction with the general teaching of Jesus—surely the soundest canon of interpretation; who hath ears to hear, let him hear, he said (Matt. xiii. 9), and take heed what ye hear (Mark iv. 24), or, how ye hear (Luke viii. 18); whosoever hath, to him shall be given and he shall have more abundance; but whosoever hath not, from him shall be taken away even that he hath (Matt. xiii. 12). What do such passages suggest, if not that, in the very construction of the world as God made it and wanted it, we must reckon with the danger of losing an unused faculty, the certainty of sin working itself out in the decline and depravation of the effective elements of nature and character, and the rejection of the unfit (a doctrine more often applied to-day to the physical aspects of life than to the spiritual)—and conversely that we may count on the growth of a man's aptitudes and faculties, and the widening of his scope, as the certain result of his using God's gifts?

Behind all this, what does Jesus suggest by the care with which he draws the old-fashioned servant? Is it not a reminder that life rests on the training of the imagination, or vision? Is it not, taken with others of his lessons, a warning against the realization of things by halves—against the danger, clear everywhere, but in the most serious region of all, the spiritual, far more significant, of being content with an un-thought-out, an unrealized life? Carlyle used to like to quote Goethe's lines from the *Generalbeichte:*

> Uns vom Halben zu entwöhnen
> Und im Ganzen, Guten, Schönen,
> Resolut zu leben.

So far the two teachers agree. But Jesus has the wider and deeper survey. What of unrealized spiritual endowment and opportunity, of unrealized carelessness in things of eternal moment, of good and evil half known and largely taken for granted? Is that life—before the bright keen eyes of the teacher from Nazareth? Or what of an un-thought-out Christ, known more or less, accepted in a traditional creed, and never "brought into our business and bosom," but left in half knowledge? Is not the

THE TALENTS

weakness of our modern Christianity precisely this—that we are content with the slack imagination, with sheer half knowledge, dim, lack-lustre and dead, where Jesus Christ is concerned—that we "make nothing of him"?

The parable points to the possibility of an intenser life, a quicker imagination, a fuller surrender of all the powers to the interests of the Master—a braver acceptance of hostile environment—a gayer and bolder snatching of opportunities—incessant development, till the servant of Christ, whatever the call, however novel or odd the situation, will know instinctively what to do. Instinct in art and in life is not an accidental thing, a gift that one has or has not. It is psychologically as probable that the faculty comes from the wish or the purpose to use it, as the other way; without doubt the developed faculty does, and that, after all, is the one that counts. The Christian instinct is the outcome of experience and thought, so deep, so inwoven with the whole man, as to be hardly conscious, but always real and effective—the outcome of a progressive surrender to Christ and an active and increasing association with him.

At the back of it all is the king in the parable—a Herod in this case, but a Herod with quick eyes for the kind of merit he prefers, who likes a man of force, and rewards him with chance after chance. It is not straining the story to say that it suggests another Master, with the same quick eyes for the type of man that *he* likes, who loves energy and reality and character, and who assuredly is never long in coming and clapping his man on the back and having him up higher for better service and closer intimacy.

VII

THE LAST EVENING

It is curious to compare the accounts given by St. John and by the Synoptists of the last evening spent by Jesus with his disciples. From the days when Tatian in the second century made the first written harmony of the Gospels, their readers have been apt to combine the data of all four evangelists in a composite picture which sometimes is distinct from that given by any one of them. As our common literary habits are uncritical, and as the blending of historical narrative is one of the most delicate tasks of historical criticism, it comes upon us with something of a surprise, or even shock, to find how the reconstructions we make for ourselves deviate from our sources. Professor Kirsopp Lake's book on the Resurrection set out the several accounts separately and clearly, and one reader at least owned to him what a revelation the book had been to him of his own inattention; and the brilliant author confessed to the same experience.

Everybody familiar with the New Testament from childhood, as so many of us are, tends to associate the last night with two things, the institution of the Lord's Supper and the discourse that begins "Let not your heart be troubled"—the four chapters of St. John that concluded with the prayer. Yet, at least, three controversies of some moment have turned upon these. On what night, the Passover night or that before it, was this gathering held, with all the momentous doings that followed it? What is the historical authority or purpose of John's gospel? And, most serious and perhaps most difficult of all, did Jesus design and enjoin an institution, a memorial rite, a sacrament or a simple habit of self-reminder—or anything at all—when he broke the bread and gave the cup? Or is his action interpreted by very early church practice, and his language coloured, naturally and guilelessly, by the associations that grew up with that practice? These questions are asked, and the answers are not very easy to find; in fact, as often happens with fundamental questions, their difficulty is only discovered by study, the first result of which is a sense of growing confusion. For once it may be possible to leave them for a while on one side and confine ourselves to watching our Lord, so far as we can, in the narrative of St. Luke. The boldest expositor must confess that there are things in the Lucan account which perplex him. But, honestly recognizing particulars that baffle us and reserving judgment on the institution or non-institution of a memorial or a sacrament, can we address ourselves to a problem less contro-

THE LAST EVENING

versial, but hardly less significant, and ask what help the data of Luke give us to discover the mind of our Lord and its movements during the hours of this strange last night? One or two particulars will be borrowed from the other Synoptists, but not such as add new features to the story; they will serve to develop what we already have in St. Luke.

I found, in studying the character of Jesus as the Gospels give it to us, that some of his most striking pieces of self-revelation come in Luke's chapter (xxii.) which describes the last evening; and it was not for some time that I saw the significance of this. Some of them are sayings which bear the stamp of genuineness upon them—too loosely connected with the texture of the story to be required by the narrative, and too susceptible of unorthodox interpretation to have been invented, or to have been kept unless their attestation was very strong. They have the marks of being the authentic recollections of someone who was present—like so much else in the gospels, the indelible memories of moments of great psychological interest, when the listener's mind was startled into great attention. Again and again the Gospels give us episodes, so short, so vivid, and (when we really understand the men and the period), so obviously startling that it is plain they rank with those unforgettable impressions of scenes and words that life gives to every one of us—impressions very deep and enduring that keep their sharp edges, the *ipsissima verba,* as long as we live.

It has been held, and there is something in the suggestion, that in his last week or two of life Jesus took precautions not to be assassinated in quiet. The narrative makes it quite plain that he expects betrayal and death; a public death it shall be. As a rule we interpret his foreknowledge too rigidly, and ignore the processes by which he learnt to forecast the future—processes made quite plain by the author of the Epistle to the Hebrews, who says that Jesus learnt by suffering. Then, for a time not specified, he learns the mind of Judas, by suffering—perhaps from the days when, after Peter's confession at Cæsarea, he speaks publicly of crosses to be carried by those who follow him, and Judas, more quickly than the rest, sees what he means and realizes his own mistake in following him. The souring of such a nature must have been particularly painful to Jesus, the sensitiveness of whose spirit is another thing from the softness which painters give him—another thing altogether, and more closely bound up with his mental and spiritual greatness, the organ of all his apprehension. We habitually under-estimate the passion of Christ by losing sight of the days and weeks that led to the cross.

What a flood of light falls on his mind and his feeling when, realizing something of what these weeks had meant to him in pain and strain, in the

THE LAST EVENING

growing sense of betrayal and of the horror of his end, we read the quiet words: "With desire I have desired to eat this passover with you before I suffer" (Luke xxii. 15). The expression is no more Greek than it is ordinary English, but it is an attempt, one of several of the kind made by Luke, to represent a Semitic idiom which expresses an action in an intensive form.[1] "I have longed, above everything, to have this meal with you, before—before *it*." It is a cry from the heart, from friend to friends, at a moment of supreme solitude and anxiety. Above everything he has wished to spend his last evening with them; it may be, to make the last effort to lay bare his mind and purpose to them, to get them at last to understand him; certainly, to have their support, their presence with him at the crisis, the staying-power of love and friendship. A little later in the chapter, the thought recurs in a very signal sentence: "Ye are they that have continued with me in my temptations" (xxii. 28). Temptation is a keyword in this chapter (xxii. 28, 40, 46), and it is linked with companionship in his thought, the danger with the safeguard. It is a revelation of his nature; like Paul, he is sensitive to being alone.[2] It is the more significant because we read of his spending long hours alone in prayer. But in temptation he

---

[1] *Cf.* Acts vii. 34, I have seen, I have seen (Greek: having seen I saw); Acts v. 28 (Greek: with charging we charged you).
[2] *Cf.* 2 Cor. ii. 13, vii. 5-7.

has found genuine help in the presence of the friends who do not understand him, who miss his ideas and think on a different plane, but who quite conspicuously like him and enjoy him and believe in him, and more—who are *with him,* his own and available for him. The two sayings, then, taken together show something of what he is undergoing—temptation, inner solitude, and an intense craving to have them with him once again when he needs them more than ever. This self-revelation, further, is an element in his gift of binding men to himself; the outgoing and craving of a strong rich nature is part of its appeal, it draws men and holds them. In weaker characters it sometimes has that effect; more here, in the stronger, such a demand for what men can give, coming with incomparable gifts to them, is one secret of his power.[1] What a reaction it must have produced in their minds to learn that in his dark hours they had done something for him; they had never guessed it, and now he told them. And his telling of the past shows what he is undergoing now.

At this point Luke sets the much-discussed reference to the cup and the bread. We shall not here add to the discussion, beyond noting it as remarkable that between the injunction as to the bread ("this do in remembrance of me") and the comparison of

[1] I am tempted to quote, but content myself by referring the reader to the passage in Browning's "Flight of the Duchess," beginning, "It is our life at thy feet we throw."

THE LAST EVENING

the cup with the shedding of his blood, the whole meal intervenes.

Jesus, as we saw, had felt increasingly that the development of Judas' present attitude must bring him to betrayal of his Master; and now he puts his conviction to the test. He announces that one of the disciples will betray him. Luke does not say more than that "they began to inquire among themselves which of them it was that should do this thing" (xxii. 23). Mark, whose narrative was before Luke as he wrote, has verses, which it seems strange that Luke did not keep: "And they began to be sorrowful, and to say unto him, one by one, Is it I? and another said, Is it I? And he answered and said unto them, It is one of the twelve, that dippeth with me in the dish" (Mark xiv. 19, 20). This vivid self-questioning of the men, addressed as it is to Jesus himself, is surely a revelation at once of affection and sincerity. That men do abandon their ideals and betray their friends, we all know; for Shylock and Judas and many others are potentially within us. A man with any gift of imagination and self-criticism will conceive with pain what he might do; he would prefer to go with his friend to prison and to death, but he knows his weakness. That these honest, simple, friendly men turn with this question to Jesus is another proof of the relations between them.

Meantime one swift look had told Jesus that the

worst was true; Judas was betraying him. Matthew and John represent that words passed between them. Perhaps, but if the Gospel narratives telling of Jesus' power to read character are true, as it is hard to doubt—we could almost have guessed that he had it—one glance was enough. John tells how Judas went out. Luke tacitly implies it.

At this point Luke tells us that the old contention broke out again, which of them should be greatest in the kingdom of heaven (xxii. 24; *cf.* ix. 46). Jesus tells them, with a hint of the playfulness which they knew, that the kings of the Gentiles are called Benefactors because they are so tyrannical, but things are to be otherwise with them; the world's order is to be inverted, the greatest is to be like the junior, to wait on the rest; and he adds that he himself is their servant. The reader wonders whether the passage belongs here; it would be difficult to prove that psychologically it is impossible, when we know how the minds of a family, for instance, all sharing a common tension, united in a common hope or fear, can find material for quarrel in what none of them care about—a proof more of strain than of anything else. If the contention arose, as Luke says, there was a charming tact in the way Jesus took to end it—proof at once of a heart at leisure from itself and a genuine knowledge of what his friends really were. It is here that he tells them how they had helped him. Cicero once wrote to a lawyer friend who was for the time in Cæsar's camp in Gaul, that he knew his friend's vanity—he would rather be consulted by Cæsar than fairly gilded by him. Of course, and which of them would not rather have helped Jesus in work or difficulty than have judged a tribe of Israel without him? There is an idealism in men, and Jesus knew it and touched it. What we are to make of the promise of thrones and dominions after this, depends on how we interpret Jesus and on the weight we lay on his statement that the men have stood by him in temptation. The verses may be due to confusion, to the mixing of stories; or they may genuinely belong here, in which case we shall have to decide whether to take them literally as they stand and suppose Jesus to be still on a low plane of Messianism—lower than, at any rate, some of the apocalyptic writers who transcended an Israelite millennium; or to suppose that Jesus used words in his own way and was understood by his friends as he knew he would be. Three ways of explanation are open, and all one need add is that literalism has never been a profitable interpreter of genius, least of all in this case. Whatever he said and whatever he meant, if the paragraph be taken as a whole, its effect is to associate Master and disciple in the past and the present, and to hint that the relation is to continue wherever they are.

Luke next tells us of the memorable words in the

singular person addressed to Peter[1]—"Simon, Simon, behold! Satan demanded you that he might sift you (plural) as wheat; but I prayer for thee that thy faith fail not; and thou, when thou comest back, strengthen thy brethren" (Luke xxii. 31, 32). Jesus, like John Bunyan and others who have had the gift of interesting listeners and readers, had the habit of seeing things in pictures; and here he seems to suggest the scene at the beginning of Job and another in the book of Zechariah (ch. iii.). Satan comes into the presence of God and stands with an insistent demand on the one hand, and opposite him is Jesus at prayer. To translate that "Satan obtained you by asking" with the margin of the Revised Version is possible but not necessary, so far as the Greek goes; it seems, however, bad theology and bad psychology. Satan never really "obtains" anyone except by asking the man himself; and there is no suggestion that he has obtained the eleven. If it is urged that he "obtained" Job under certain conditions, there appears to be nothing of a parallel here. From the lips of so clear a thinker and so genuine a friend, what can the passage mean but peril at hand, once more that reminder of temptation which fills the chapter? "But I prayed for thee" are surely words that the man, to whom they were spoken, could never forget. They show how Jesus individu-

[1] Here something of what has already appeared in "The Jesus of History" is handled again.

THE LAST EVENING

alized men, and they tell us how he had been spending the mountain nights of prayer. Let a man picture it with his own name set for Simon's, and reflect that Jesus sat alone with God, thinking out with God "my name"; what would it mean to him? And Jesus spoke so to Peter, not without foresight of what was to be that night, and the repentance of his friend. No wonder he bound men to him!

The night was to bring Peter shame enough; and Jesus foresaw it. He had not lived with the child of impulse for nothing. With Peter it would be hit or miss, the bull's eye or off the target; if he went wrong, it would be wildly wrong; if he took to denial, there would be no limits in his denial, he could not do it once and let it alone. And Jesus knew it, and knew too the other side of the man's nature, loyal for all his spells of panic fear;[1] and before the fall occurs, he predicts the certain return and calls him to great service. He knew his man. The warning is lost on him, and he lapses into his superlatives on the spot. When the bad moment came, he gave way, lied furiously, and fulfilled the prophecy; "and the Lord turned and looked upon Peter" (xxii. 61), and Peter "came back"; they understood one another.

The verses about the purse, the shoes, and the

[1] *Cf.* the episode at Antioch, where Peter plunged, first one way and then the other, Galat. ii. 11. Paul also knew Peter, and seems to have read him in much the same way.

sword are not very clear. They key to them seems to be lost. I do not agree in the least with one interpreter who holds that Jesus lost his head for a moment, and finds comfort in the aberration. Mark's ending of the meal, with a "hymn" (Mark xiv. 26) Luke omits, but it will none the less be genuine, and it adds a touch to the story of the companionship that we have not elsewhere. It would probably be a psalm, something with God at the centre of it.

The events in the garden are cut down by Luke or expanded by Matthew. There is again, twice over, the warning about temptation; and Luke gives us a glimpse of the solitary agony, the sweat profuse and heavy,[1] the prayer on one note. An interpolator has brought in an angel, in a verse happily lacking in some manuscripts. Mark more closely touches what happened. After an hour the strain upon Jesus grows too intense, and he rises from his knees and seeks his friends; he wants them with him in his temptation once more. He finds them asleep. Could not Peter have kept awake one hour with him? Well, he understands; they were ready enough in heart, but weary bodies overpowered their will. Even here he saves their faces and goes back to his temptation, alone and without them. This happened twice, Mark says. None of the evangelists

[1] This, however, depends on a verse which stands textually with that which brings in the angel.

THE LAST EVENING 117

comments on his story, but the reader may. It should be noted that the cup might quite easily have passed; he had only to rise from his knees and leave the garden; a night of walking, and the cup was gone—and how much else with it! He wrestles through, and alone.

At last, and it must have been in measure a relief, he catches the sound of feet and knows what they mean. He goes for the last time to the disciples, and wakes them, and the crowd is upon them. He knew that Judas had brought them, but one thing he had not foreseen. There are decencies in dishonour for some men, but others do not care about them. Judas need not have been seen; the thick heavy stems of the olive trees in the garden might have been shelter; the heavy black shadows of a night of full moon could have concealed him; but he was of a coarser make. He went directly up to Jesus to kiss him. Luke does not say with Mark and Matthew, that Judas actually did kiss Jesus. Without their accounts one would infer from Luke's turn of sentence (the infinitive of purpose) that Jesus saw what he meant to do, and saved himself from that touch. "Hail, master!" was enough. The cry breaks from Jesus, which we can believe authentic, and it reveals an unexpected humiliation and sorrow: "Judas, betrayest thou the Son of Man *with a kiss?*"

Here the scene changes and he is with his friends no more. But if the construction we have given to the data of Luke is right, and it seems natural and obvious enough, we have in the chapter a revelation of the inmost mind of Jesus. The story is not that told by St. John, but the keynote is the same. "With desire I have desired to eat this passover with you before I suffer," Luke quotes the very words of Jesus; and John long after sums it all up in a judgment—a thing as beautiful as any in his Gospel, and as true history—"Jesus . . . having loved his own which were in the world, he loved them unto the end" (xiii. 1).

VIII

THE WRITER TO THE HEBREWS

I

The Council of Trent decided among other things that St. Paul wrote the Epistle to the Hebrews. There was a long tradition in support of that decision, going back to Clement of Alexandria, who, however, lives in virtue of other gifts than his criticism. But there is as good tradition warranting doubt of the ascription. Origen, a junior contemporary of Clement, and a much better judge in such things, holds that if Paul wrote the epistle, some Greek must have edited it, some amanuensis; but he concludes, "who wrote the epistle, God knows." So early was the style of the writer felt by those sensitive to such things. Later scholars in our own day analyse the vocabulary and find marked differences from Paul. The whole construction of the letter, however, all but cries aloud that Paul never wrote it; when did Paul ever keep to so even a level of graceful language, or so consecutively adhere to a train of thought? Paul neither had the training of this writer nor wanted it;[1] he is far swifter

[1] Compare 1 Cor. ii. 4.

in mind and intuition, sees things suddenly in a flash, and has a divine gift of being centrifugal, even if he always does come back to his ultimate centre. Nor are Paul's main ideas, nor his general outlook, to be found in this writer.

Many have guessed at the name of the author, Apollos, Silas, Barnabas, and even Priscilla have been credited with the authorship, but the claims of Aristarchus, Timothy, and Onesimus are at present just as solid. We know nothing whatever of the literary capacity of any one of them. Apollos could preach with power; Aristarchus was a brave and loyal comrade; Barnabas was Jove-like, at least compared with the Mercurial Paul.[1] And there it ends. We have not enough knowledge to ascribe the letter to any person named in the New Testament; it is equally plain that he is none of the writers who wrote the other New Testament books; and we have no option but to leave his name where Origen left it, in the knowledge of God.

The name does not greatly matter, though it would be convenient in speaking of the epistle and its writer to know it. But it is not the only book that has come down to us without a name and yet full of an autobiography. The date is established by the free quotation from the book as one accepted which we find in the letter of Clement of Rome, who wrote about A.D. 95. The race of the author

[1] Acts xiv. 12.

is less easy to decide. It is urged that he knew the Old Testament well, but in Greek, following the Septuagint even in its blunders; that his knowledge of Judaism is book-knowledge; that he writes apparently for people whose acquaintance with Jewish law and ceremony would be helped by more explanation than we should imagine Jews to require; and he has no such sentiment about Israel as we find in Paul. If he was familiar with the methods of Philo in handling the Old Testament, so were others who used them and were undoubtedly Gentiles, like Clement of Alexandria. He may have been a proselyte, as Justin Martyr and Tatian were; and Justin had an extraordinary knowledge of the Old Testament. His Greek, Hellenistic as it may be, is purer and more genial, better every way than that of any other New Testament writer; and one may be forgiven for thinking that his tone of mind goes with it, and that he writes more like a Gentile than a Jew. No one would think of him instinctively as an Athenian; Alexandria suggests itself—probably from the influence of Philo; but his place of abode or of origin must be left unknown. It is equally impossible to say to whom his letter was directed, if it was a letter at all, and not a tract or pamphlet thrown into letter form.[1]

That he was a man of culture is clear, a real

[1] The reference to Timothy (xiii. 23) suggests the letter; but the last four verses may be a mere note that was sent with the document (perhaps to one set of friends).

Hellenist. That he read the Septuagint, and liked Philo's exegesis, we have seen. And it is surely not going too far to feel in his pages the direct or indirect influence of Plato. Whether Paul studied with Stoic teachers at Tarsus (which is doubtful), or read Stoic books (which is doubtful), his vocabulary and his ideas show Stoic terms and Stoic thought. "Nature" was the very foundation of Stoic teaching, and "conscience" was a coinage of that school; and the man who uses the terms, and uses them with meaning and intelligence, can be said to have come under Stoic influence. It is much easier to suppose that the writer to the Hebrews had a personal acquaintance of his own with Plato; but whether this is so or not, it is hardly fanciful to catch a reminiscence of Plato's parable of the cave and the men bound in it who saw not things, nor models of things, but shadows of models,[1] when we read that the law had "a shadow of good things to come and not the very image of the things" (Hebrews x. 1). It is noticeable, too, that while the Gospels speak of the Kingdom of God (or of heaven), for this Greek-minded man, the Kingdom becomes a city, which men seek; and in both ideas he has Plato, one feels, in his mind, if not the words at least the influence of Plato. "Plato," says Dr. James Adam,

[1] Plato, "Rep.," vii. 514 foll. Though Plato does not use εἰκόνα of the models, the word actually comes immediately in his text, meaning "parable" or "likeness," and Jowett translates it "image."

"in the *Republic* is looking for a *civitas dei,* new heavens and new earth, *in which righteousness dwelleth* (2 Peter iii. 13); and indeed, as the argument unfolds itself, we behold the originally "Hellenic city' gradually changing into a celestial commonwealth a παράδειγμα ἐν οὐρανῷ, as Plato himself at last confesses it to be";[1] and in his commentary on the *Republic* (ix. 592 B) Adam refers to more than one passage of this epistle (xi. 16, xii. 23, xiii. 14);[2] Plato again puts the idea of *Weltflucht* before his followers; we must direct our flight yonder with all speed, away from this world of sense, and the way of escape is to grow like God (*Theætus* 176 A). Closely similar is the picture of the search for a city given by Lucian in his caustic parody, the *Hermotimus*. It is perhaps not irrelevant to note how this Platonized city of God has come down through St. Augustine, the poet Spenser, and John Bunyan; and the last, we may be sure, drew all his Platonism from the epistle to the Hebrews, city and pilgrim and world-flight. It is something to have given the world of letters an eternal interpretation; it means that the man who does it has the feeling for ideas and the instinct for language. It also illustrates the view that the mind of Jesus never got real expression in words and terms, till it was linked

---

[1] Adam, "Vitality of Platonism," p. 65.
[2] Plato's word *demiurge* appears in Heb. xi. 10; and other philosophic terms are quoted to establish the writer's "notable predilection" for them.

with Greek. The city of God has been far more potent a conception and aspiration than the original kingdom, especially since the Apocalyptist gave it a name, the New Jerusalem; and he, we should remember, wrote at a later date than our author, whether he knew him or not.

There then is our scholar, and we have found him in his library. Others have tracked him to the school in which he studied; they have noted his modes of speech and given them the technical names which they bore in the schools of rhetoric. We need not linger over these, but it is easy to see that he learnt to write and was practised in expression. There is nothing ragged in his style; his ideas are ordered, his transitions well made, and his keynotes as they recur come in naturally and with force.

He is a student of human nature, analytical of his own mind and feelings, on the whole mistrustful of himself and his impulses. He is conscious of the limitations of man's outlook; God may have put all things under man as the psalmist (Psalm viii.) had said, "but now we see not yet all things put under him" (ii. 8). He feels the need of "an anchor of the soul, safe and firm," an anchor in the world of the unseen (vi. 19). He emphasizes the craving for a conscience purified from a dead past to be able to serve a living God (ix. 14); a man needs a full assurance of faith that his heart is "sprinkled from evil conscience," rid, that is, of consciousness of evil (x. 22); and in his postscript, he hopes or even trusts he has a good conscience, at least, he wishes to live honourably in all things (xiii. 18). The failure of Judaism was that its sacrifices never did set a man free from consciousness of sin (x. 2). A note like this does not recur in a man's writing—in the writing of a man so skilled and so deliberate—without significance.

He is sensitive to the insidiousness of temptation, and speaks with tenderness of the tempted in their need of help, and with gratitude to Jesus especially for his sharing the burden of temptation, to Jesus who knew it in the days of his flesh in bitter experience, and helps his friends when they are in need (ii. 18, iv. 16). The sympathy of Jesus in this matter he sets out as movingly as Paul himself (ii. 18, iv. 15). It is noticeable in this connexion that he uses the name Jesus by itself, more than other New Testament writers outside the Gospels. What his special temptations were, we may be able to guess later on. He knew also something of the fear of death, a fear contributory, Aristotle would tell us, to a genuine manhood, but a fear, which, our writer knows, may keep a man paralysed his whole life through (ii. 15). Above all he is afraid of apostasy. He realizes vividly what it means in the end, and he fears God; "it is a fearful thing to fall into the hands of the living God" (x. 31; *cf.* x. 26–31, vi. 6, xii. 17). He mistrusts himself, as we shall see, in a world where it is so fatally easy to drift. A "sombre" element has been noted in his conception of God; his view of sin and punishment, of inevitable consequences, is as stringent as Plato's. As little as the great Athenian teacher can he believe that men may play as they please with God's laws. If this is sombre, then he is sombre; but experience contributes such a character to the mind of a man who looks within and remembers God. There was, as we shall see, a good deal in his environment to give a serious, if not a dark, tinge to thought; yet his dominant note we shall find to be one of hope (vi. 18, 19).

Though he has read Plato and learnt from him, he is not greatly interested in philosophy or theology. He has a theology, a Christology at any rate, which is the outcome of experience and thought; but it is not that of the professed philosopher. In Philo he had fallen in with a bad school of exegesis, but he never loses his real meaning in subtleties;[1] he retains enough of the Greek mind to know the difference between substance and shadow; his allegories do not obscure real issues for him. He is simple, sincere and direct; he speaks out of experience and he thinks clearly; he knows whom he has believed, and has a straightforward faith in Jesus. He is prepared to take risks both in life and thought for him,

[1] Unless we except the play with the two meanings of *diatheke,* covenant and testament.

to try a new and bold experiment in religion, and he looks forward, in the old Athenian way,[1] with eyes open and head cool, to a very probable martyrdom. If he is afraid of his own weakness, and afraid in another sense of God, he "will not fear what man shall do unto me" (xiii. 6).

II

The man is a scholar, a stylist, a man of books; and somehow he has been led into the region of experiment. He tells us nothing of his history, and it is impossible to guess what brought him into the Christian community. But we find him there and engaged simultaneously in two great questions, one in the sphere of religion, the other of character. He has to find a justification for the Christian faith in its great departure from all the world's religious traditions, and to combat all the temptations to inertia and drift that beset the life of man.

It is hard for us after so many centuries of Christianity to realize how strangely Judaism, and still more so the Christian faith, struck the world. This man's contemporary Tacitus made an epigram of Jewish religion, a temple without god or image, an empty shrine, non-existent mysteries.[2] The vulgar, and not they alone, dubbed the Christians atheists; they so obviously were—what else could they be,

[1] *Cf.* Thucydides, ii. 40.
[2] Tacitus, "Histories," v. 9.

who would not worship their neighbours' gods and had none of their own? The absence of intelligible ritual provoked imagination, and a dirty fancy found rites for people who had none, in the legends of Œdipus and Tantalus.

Religion had always implied temple, or at least altar, and it could not exist without priest and sacrifice. In fact, as our author says or quotes: "Without shedding of blood there is no remission" (ix. 22). To the ancient, with certain exceptions, the sacrifice was the essential thing in religion, the one means of approach to gods, which was inevitable and infallible. The exceptions were the prophets of Israel and some of the philosophers of Greece, who saw plainly enough that to God it was the heart and its change or development that really mattered; at best the sacrifice could only be a symbolic representation of this approach of heart and nature, and between minds, such as those that they saw God's must be and man's ought to be, symbols were not needed.

It is an irony that has befallen other writers, that what they have written has been taken to support exactly what they attacked.[1] Our writer has been mishandled, and has become, in the hands of his interpreters, the prime advocate of a system of ideas which he clearly rejected, as if the Christian faith were only valid if it could be expressed in the terms

[1] *e.g.* St. John vi. 56, 63.

THE WRITER TO THE HEBREWS

of the religions it was to abolish. He has been interpreted as giving a sacerdotal and sacrificial character to the work of Christ, when it is fairer to hold that he maintains the work of Christ to supersede all sacerdotal and sacrificial conceptions.

True, he takes in turn priest (vii. 18–27), sacrifice (viii. 3), sanctuary (ix. 1), and altar (xiii. 10), and in turn identifies Jesus with each, or more really finds that, whatever function each of these things was supposed to discharge, Jesus does discharge in a much more thorough way, once and for all. An illustration may serve here. Tacitus says that Augustus "drew to himself all the functions of Senate, magistrates and laws";[1] Cicero after the death of Cæsar had written to Plancus (of all people), "Be the Senate yourself"—a shorter way of saying something of the same kind. When our writer speaks of Jesus as priest (vii. 24–28), passing through the veil, viz., his flesh (x. 20), by the sacrifice of himself (ix. 26), with his *own* blood (ix. 12; xiii. 12), entering into the holy place (ix. 12); when he says we have an altar whereof they have no right to eat which serve the tabernacle (xiii. 10); it is plain that an educated Greek cannot think of these terms as denoting anything literal whatever. He is using analogy and illustration, and is no more to be taken literally than Jesus is, when he says that the kingdom of heaven is like a net in the sea, and leaven

[1] Tacitus, "Annals," i. 2.

in the meal, and a man who found a treasure, and a king marrying his son. The images are not to be combined, consistently with sanity; and he was entirely sane and very clear. What the priest did, or was supposed to do, partially and ineffectually, for it needed constant repetition, Jesus did once for all. If shedding of blood is your *sine qua non* in religion, *his* blood was shed. With the prophets and Jesus historically behind him, it is hardly to be supposed that the writer really conceived of God as a being not to be satisfied without blood. And having begun to play with analogies, he adds the veil after the manner of the school, which surely shows how little he took all his analogies as expressing necessary modes of religion. A little study of Clement of Alexandria will show of what daring fancies the school was capable, without loss of intellectual clearness. It was a later and less Alexandrian age, more legal in training, more literalist in temper, that riveted on the Church allegories which greater men conceived and used, and dropped as they passed on to things deeper and more essential.

When he comes to hard fact, our writer is perfectly plain as to his meaning. Animal sacrifice is absolutely futile; and any modern Christian, who has seen it, knows what the writer means, and how entirely right he is. "It is not possible that the blood of bulls and goats should take away sins" (x. 4); they are offered continually, which is in itself proof that they leave the conscience polluted and unhappy (x. 2), and they never do take away sins (x. 11). He is only reasserting what the great prophets had said, and the proof of it lies in his citation of the central thought of Jeremiah's message—the promise of the new covenant unlike the old in every way, non-sacrificial, inward, effectual (viii. 8-12; Jeremiah xxxi. 31 ff.). Nor is this the only passage of the Old Testament he quotes; for he draws from Psalm xl. verses to prove that God is approached not in sacrifices but through the will. The ultimate religion must be one of the will, and it must be one that gets rid of sin forever.

As for the law of Moses, he does not find it in such direct antithesis to the Gospel as Paul does. To him it is like the shadows seen by Plato's prisoners in the cave, a mass of inexact and therefore misleading pictures, which do indeed correspond with reality but at a remove—not images, but shadows, vague and uncertain, things one can be glad to be done with. All rites become useless and obsolete when peace of conscience is gained, never to be lost again. The shadows are nothing, when the reality comes. The law vanishes away, grown old and obsolete (viii. 13).

The reality is the bright personality of Jesus. He moves out of the realm of shadows and types into the highest and most real man can divine. It is Jesus doing the will of God, who does away with shadows

—expressing and fulfilling God's nature, the "express image" (*charactêr*) of God (i. 3). The point is a difficult one to make clear; but in spite of Philonian exegesis his emphasis is plainly on the relation of Jesus to God, the obedience rendered by Jesus to God, the identity of will, the entrance of Christ forever into the presence of God once for all, his seat at the right hand of God. We touch here concepts not to be validly translated into the symbolism of Mosaic law; and the appeal to the fortieth psalm takes the whole matter to a higher level. We have not yet a final account of "the work" of Christ; but as Christendom has entered into the mind of Jesus, it has moved further and further away from the whole range of ideas represented by sacrifice and altar. Our writer has to treat of sacrifice and altar, but he makes it evident that he himself thought essentially in other terms, or at the least had entered a train of thought which implied other categories. It is impossible for one long familiar with his Greek cadences on the priesthood, the intercessorship, of Christ not to love the thought; and it may be inferred that he loved it himself. One must have some language in which to express the deepest feelings; and if our writer is steadily bringing his readers over to a new outlook, he still has to use a language that will stir their hearts. At the centre of every conception of priesthood is the idea of effective relation with God. The old priesthood, the old sacrifices, failed to bring this about for men; Jesus has done it once for all. If sacrifice expresses this achievement, he is our sacrifice; if priesthood, he is our priest; but none of these terms, nor all of them taken together, really express him. This our writer has seen, and it is misreading him to make him the pillar of a mode of exposition, the fundamental ideas of which he roundly calls obsolete.

III

Side by side with the theological problem of relation with God on new lines, our writer feels the practical problem of the management of life. Those who never read the great books do not know their appeal; a man who never handles great ideas, who pursues no absorbing study, has little notion of how they can occupy mind and life, and how one can wake with a start to find one has drifted from one's centre. Attention means inattention; and a scholar will realize with shame how the great and high interests of history and thought and science may so control him as to leave him inattentive to God. There are other things that lead to neglect (ii. 3), to drift (ii. 1), to coming short (iv. 1), to turning aside or wavering (x. 23), to dulness (*nôthroi*, vi. 12) and to forgetfulness (xii. 5), and thence to fall (iv. 11) and refusal (xii. 25). It is to be noted how this warning against inattention, with its insidious and unnoticed dangers, comes periodically through his writing, like a motif in a piece of music. Nor this only, but interwoven with it are other motifs, the emphasis on attention, on faith, and on the power of Christ. To track them as they come gives one a new sense of his gift in writing, as, not schematically, but naturally and (it might seem) almost unconsciously he recurs to his great notes and makes them felt, felt more than we at first have realized.

The real danger before the Christian was apostasy, the final rejection of salvation, the acme of all that stains and ruins conscience, the doom a man writes for himself in a universe where God rules and where God, like a consuming fire (xii. 29, quoting Deut. iv. 24), destroys all that would frustrate His will, burns up the refuse and the waste of the world. No one would deliberately undertake to tread the Son of God underfoot (x. 29); no one would deliberately choose a lifetime of fearful expectation of judgment (x. 27). *Nemo repente fuit turpissimus,* says a Latin poet, more or less contemporary, and no such reader of the soul as our writer. The greatest disasters of crime, of falsity, of apostasy, are those into which men drift. It is so easy to drift; and when suddenly the government calls for the Christian's blood (xii. 4), a man may have faltered, may have been startled into denial, before he is conscious of what he is doing.

"Consider" (xii. 3), he keeps saying, "attend" (ii. 1), "study" (vii. 4), "remark" (iii. 1). His eleventh chapter is an appeal to history, to memory and the challenge of great examples. Elsewhere he bids his friends recall their own experience—those earlier days, when after the great enlightenment they had great practice or training in suffering; when men made exhibitions of them with taunts and persecution and robbery (x. 32–34). Above all this they must get their eyes on Jesus Christ and keep them there.

As a practical step, the simple and obvious means of keeping touch with the great story of Jesus and of concentrating thought upon him, he recommends steady adherence to the Christian community—"not forsaking the assembling of ourselves together" (x. 25). He emphasizes in the same verse preaching:—a Greek of the intellectual type, he prefers teaching and thought, the touch of mind with mind, to sacraments. He does not use of the Church the splendid language of Paul, still less the falutin of some second-century Christians. To him its real value is that of a community, a *Gemeinde,* a society, of similar experience, similar needs, and a common faith in Jesus. But even Paul hardly surpasses the picture he draws of the Church invisible—"Ye are come unto Mount Sion, and unto the city of the living God, the heavenly Jerusalem, and to an innumerable company of angels, to the general assembly and church of the firstborn which are written in heaven, and to God the Judge of all, and to the spirits of just men made perfect, and to Jesus" (xii. 22, 23). The angels here may be of Hebrew or Philonian origin; the rest is Greek. The "general assembly" is the *panêgyris* of the Olympian games; the "Church" is the *ecclesia* of glorious memories of freedom; and the citizens are registered in heaven, their rights assured. And he completes his picture of the Church with the presence of God and—in culmination—Jesus named by his earthly name.

The need is urgent, the peril is imminent. Men must have their minds in working order; they must concentrate attention; above all they must have faith in the unseen. It is easy to lose this faith if one lives in study or even in comfort, if one lets attention wander to the pleasant and the fugitive. One feels that to a day like ours, the writer has a special message, and that his emphasis on the history of spiritual experience is our *via prima salutis*. The idealists cut odd figures in this world; did not Cleon in Athens, five hundred years before, touch them off? men "in bondage to whatever is exotic, to every new paradox, contemptuous of the ordinary, seeking something else (so to say) than the conditions under which we live, and unable to take in what stares them in the face."[1] Our author says very much the same thing about them, but with a sympathetic tone: "These all died in their faith, they did not receive what was promised, they only saw it afar off[2] and hailed it with a cheer, they admitted that they were foreigners and aliens on earth. Those who say such things declare plainly that they are still seeking[3] a country; and truly if they had remembered the country whence they came they might have had opportunity to go back to it. But in point of fact they desire[4] a better country, one in heaven.[5] So God is not ashamed to be called their God, for He has a city ready for them" (xi. 13–16). So far, for us who are still on earth, the only justification for the idealists is to be got from experience and from history, and to history and "your own experience" this scholar goes. God, he maintains, is on the side of the idealists; the City of God is built, is ready and waiting, and some men get a glimpse of it and salute it from afar nad set out for it—"seeking something different from the terms on which we live." In human history, he sees, it is the idealists who have done everything; God is not ashamed of them, He

[1] Thucydides iii. 38; I have given alternative renderings of the first phrase. *Cf.* J. B. Bury, "Ancient Greek Historians," p. 115.
[2] "If the city had only been near at hand and plain for all to see," says Lucian in his "Hermotimus" 25, "but it lies far away!"
[3] *Epizêtein,* almost Cleon's word, *zêtein.*
[4] *Oregontai,* a good Thucydidean word.
[5] Plato again.

has vindicated them again and again; they have subdued kingdoms, achieved righteousness, got what was promised them, triumphed over brute beasts and brute men, and so forth; why should I try to paraphrase his Hymn for all Idealists (xi. 32-40)? The last note of it is a splendid challenge; for all they did and achieved, God has something better for us, we are needed to complete them.

History is full of comfort and inspiration, but he has something more to add.

IV

We have seen how our writer's great keynotes recur. One of them escapes nobody who reads the Epistle—his emphasis on remembering Jesus, considering Jesus, taking note of Jesus. For him, in the long run, in thought, and in life or death, everything turns on Jesus; every issue comes down to the practical concentration on Jesus, the eyes fixed on him in the race-course of life (xii. 1), and everything here and hereafter staked upon faith in him.

He might vie with Paul in the splendour and intensity of the names he has for the Son of God, with all that such Sonship implies—crowned with glory and honour (ii. 9), entering the holy place with eternal redemption for us (ix. 12, no symbol, but the very presence of God, ix. 24), and not alone like the high priest of the Jews but bringing his friends emboldened with him (x. 19), sitting on the right hand of God (i. 4, x. 12). Christ is "the brightness [1] of God's glory and the express image of his nature" (i. 3); he laid the foundations of the earth, and the heavens are the work of his hands (i. 10), and he upholds all things by his word of power (i. 3); he is the firstborn of God (i. 6). Not all these terms and expressions are new in religious thought; the reader may think of Philo, perhaps of the Stoics.[2]

But the glow and the affection with which he sweeps together everything that may help to bring Christ in his greatness and glory, flamingly into the heart of every man, these are new; and they tell us something of the man—a great deal, in fact, of his experience and his passion.

For this supreme Christ is no abstract dogma like the *Logos* of the philosophers. The names which our author gives to Christ in his relations with men are even more moving—a High Priest holy, harmless, undefiled, out of the category of sinners, with no need every day to purge away his own sins before he can deal with ours (vii. 26); Mediator of a new covenant, that better covenant which Jeremiah foresaw, under which every man will have God's laws written in his heart (instead of the defiling impulses we know now), and all men shall know God (viii. 6, xii. 24); the Surety of this covenant (vii.

---

[1] *Apaugasma*, a word from Wisdom, vii. 26; see p. 158.
[2] A hint of Stoic phrase in ii. 10.

22); the Author and Perfecter of the faith (xii. 2); our Fore-runner (vi. 20), and (in language perhaps borrowed from our Lord's parable recorded by Luke, for John's Gospel was yet to write) "the great Shepherd of the sheep" (xiii. 20). Every phrase again speaks of experience and feeling. The eternal Son of God is the pledge and guaranty for the salvation of men, mediator, fore-runner, intelligible to them and interpreter and representative of them; "He ever liveth to make intercession for them" (vii. 25).

What differentiates him from Paul and other New Testament writers, apart from the evangelists, and at the same time gives him an appeal to ourselves, is the clear view he has of the sufferings of Jesus. He is himself a tempted and troubled man, and it is a help to him to realize how much of his experience repeats that of Jesus, and how much more of the same kind Jesus had. He keeps his eyes fixed on Jesus, as he puts it; and when nature fails to show all things subjected to man, "We see Jesus for the suffering of death crowned with glory and honour, that he by the grace of God should taste death for every man," we see him "perfected by suffering" (ii. 9, 10). Men are haunted with the fear of death, so Jesus tastes it for them and frees them from their fear (ii. 15). Men reel and sicken under temptation; Jesus knew temptation, and in virtue of his knowledge (gained in suffering) he can help the tempted (ii. 18). He is flesh and blood like the rest of us (ii. 14), and is taught by obedience (v. 8). Our writer keeps his eyes on Jesus in Gethsemane, "when he offered up prayers and supplications, with strong crying (on God) and with tears, to him who was able to save him from death, and was heard in that he feared" (v. 7). This is a remarkable note in the early church, and it suggests autobiography. Finally, he sees Jesus in shame and contradiction carry his cross without the gates (xii. 2, xiii. 12). And the keynote of all comes back to our memory, the note with which he began; it was all done by Jesus to cleanse the conscience from sin (i. 3), to give the peace a man can only have when guilt and defilement are gone forever (ix. 14, x. 2, 14, 17, 18, 22), to bring us indeed into the presence of God (ix. 24, x. 19).

One more of his recurring notes remains, a steady, quiet, repeated insistence on the power of Jesus— *power* to help the tempted (ii. 18), *power* to sympathize with us and to understand us on the side of our weaknesses (iv. 15), *power* to have effective compassion on the ignorant and the muddled who lose themselves (v. 2), *power* to save to the uttermost (vii. 25), and (by implication) *power* to take away sin, to cleanse the conscience and to perfect (x. 10, 11, ix. 9, x. 1).

So he conceives of Jesus, and is prepared for the worst,—for a brave new experiment in religious life, 'for the utmost of temptation, and for the naked horror of earthly death. The types and fancies all go; and at last he says, in a sort of religious nihilism, that he wants nothing but Jesus. The last extremity of isolation lies "outside the camp"; outside the camp Jesus suffered in shame and loneliness; "let us go forth therefore unto him without the camp, bearing his reproach" (xiii. 13).

IX

THE HOLY SPIRIT

It is sometimes supposed that to examine the various stages of the history of an idea may lead, or must lead, to the idea being found untenable. Thus, in some men's opinion, if it can be shown that at an early stage all the religion we can find among a people was, so far as we know, associated with fetiches and taboos (to go no further), and was a matter of imperfect and invalid thought, then it is to be assumed that at all later stages the same may fairly be said of their religion. It is held that a stream cannot rise above its source; but metaphors do not always illustrate a case. A river may have many tributaries, and one of them may change the character of what we call the main stream. If a savage, for instance, be proved to associate any notion, which he so far possesses of the idea *god,* with a stone, it does not invalidate the idea to prove that the association is a wrong one. To disprove the existence of a god, more is needed than to show that men have blundered in their attribution of deity. Behind the blundering ascription, behind the confused thinking, there may lie the most dynamic of human convictions, that all life has to be associated with a powerful and persistent unseen element. To call this philosophy, and to urge that it has nothing to do with religion, is a mere matter of definition; and some thinkers, who suppose themselves liberal, fail to see that a man may be as doctrinaire and arbitrary in definition or classification as any priest or obscurantist contending for a ceremony or a dogma. Historical inquiry, like all criticism, is directed to the learning of facts and sequences and to the clearing of ideas; it cannot alter facts, though it may affect our interpretation of them. In religion as in history the facts are of more import than our theories about them; and if the investigation of the history of men's judgment upon facts lead to a clearer grasp of those facts, the presumption is that it will lead to a sounder judgment, a view of facts that may in turn stimulate to fresh experiment upon them and to further discovery.

I

When we turn to the Christian conception of the Holy Spirit, we are reminded at once that the doctrine was formulated in the first three centuries of the Church, while it still lived in a world full of animistic ideas, and depended, in a degree to us surprising, on the inherited religious and philosophical outlooks of an earlier age. We recall too that there was a Hebrew inheritance, like and yet unlike the Greek, already interpreted by non-Christians in Greek terms. Finally, we have to realize, if we can, the actual experience of the early Christian in street and home, in temple and amphitheatre, and to remember the great transformation of everything that Christ had effected for him—a transformation less evident than it would have been, if it could have been described in a wholly new language. But it is only scientific men who use wholly new language, and their terminology gets sadly perverted when it reaches the lips of ordinary people.

To modern readers, in whose minds the long drill of ages has effected some clarification, not always as valid or permanent as it seems, the dreadful confusion of ancient thought is amazing. When Homer, for instance, clearest and most lucid of poets, passes from description of life as men see it, of land and sea, home and battle, love and fear and death, and attempts to speak of the soul, we can no longer translate him with any assurance. The "souls"— or whatever the *psychai* are—of many goodly heroes are sent to Hades; "themselves" are given to dogs and birds; so the "Iliad" begins, as we remember, and it ends with the ghost of Patroclus; but whether that ghost and the dead generally have or have not, as Achilles says, *phrenes* for all their retaining *psyche* and form, who is bold enough to decide? What do the words mean?

Homer is essentially a modern. For the real ancients, as for the survivors of primitive man today, it was not clear what the *psyche* was. Are you your soul, or is it something different from you? Can *you* count on what *it* will do? Are *you* sure that *your soul* is really friendly to *you?* Then what happens when you faint or otherwise lose consciousnes in sleep or illness? Where has your soul gone? When you dream, has your soul actually reached the places about which you dream? And all the changes of mood and mind, depression, high spirits, madness, illness—how are they to be accounted for? The obvious answer was that another spirit entered the man. The language has a modern sound, but it is an inheritance from the most distant ages. Why should a man in love, or a man drunk, differ in mind and speech and action from himself under normal conditions? Surely something has *possessed* him; and there we touch a whole series of words, handed down to us from other days, and still preserving an early attempt at psychology—possession, obsession, bewitched, nympholept, with influence and enthusiasm at the end of the list, to add a respectability which they owe to a change of meaning and to forgetfulness.

Not only things so normal as love and dreams and childbirth, but every psychopathic state, and perhaps every pathological condition, was attributed to the

THE HOLY SPIRIT

occupation of the man or woman by a dæmon or a god. The dæmon physically got inside the human and produced the change of mind, the loss of reason, the poem or the baby. Even when the true nature of child-bearing was understood, the old explanation was kept to account for the second child when twins were born. So confused are the early ideas— the origin of life, the origin of death, physical factors to-day identifiable as infections, every exhilaration,—they are all attributed to one class of cause; and if we ask whether it is spiritual or physical, the distinction is simply not made, not even thought of as yet.

In the seventh and sixth centuries B. C. there was a great religious movement in Greece, associated with the name of the god Dionysus. Strange stories were told of the religious experiences, which men and especially women underwent, as the cult spread southward from Thrace,—how the worshippers gathered at night on the mountains, clad in fawn-skins and carrying ivy-wreathed wands, how they danced to the music of flutes and cymbals, how they tore living animals to pieces and ate them raw, and how a swoon would follow. These were the outward events. Men and women were stirred by the hope of union with the godhead; and in the frenzy of the dance, amid the beat of the cymbals, the god possessed them, they grew conscious of him, felt him and attained beatitude.[1] Similar phenomena [2] are recorded of many religions, and the common features are the group seized with the same idea, the stimulus, the weakening of inhibitory control, the surrender, the spread of the movement by imitation, the god-consciousness, and frequently, the same heightening of muscular power and other hypnotic effects.[3] The strange character of it all concentrated attention on it and helped its spread; and the difficulty of explaining the consciousness of contact with another life and the muscular feats, which even outsiders could verify, served to prove the truth of the explanation given—the access of a god and his entrance into his worshipper.

The description which Virgil long afterwards draws of the Sibyl, when Æneas consults her, reproduces the old belief and some of the constant accompaniments.[4]

> The sacred threshold now they trod;
> "Pray for an answer! pray! the God,"
>   She cries, "the God is nigh!"
> And as before the doors in view
> She stands, her visage pales its hue,
>   Her locks dishevelled fly.
> Her breath comes thick, her wild heart glows,
> Dilating as the madness grows,

---

[1] G. F. Moore, "History of Religion," i. 442; J. B. Bury, "History of Greece," 312.
[2] Davenport, "Primitive Traits in Religious Revivals."
[3] Plato, "Ion," 534. The Bacchanal women draw milk and honey from rivers when under the influence of Dionysus, but not when in their right mind.
[4] Virgil, "Æneid," vi. 45 f., 77 f. (Conington's translation).

THE HOLY SPIRIT

> Her form looks larger to the eye.
> Unearthly peals her deep-toned cry,
> As breathing nearer and more near
> The God comes rushing on his seer.

She bids Æneas pray, and he prays; and, as he prays, the possession becomes more complete:

> The seer, impatient of control,
>   Raves in the cavern vast
> And madly struggles from her soul
>   The incumbent power to cast:
> He, mighty Master, plies the more
> Her foaming mouth, all chafed and sore,
> Tames her wild heart with plastic hand
> And makes her docile to command.

Professor Jevons quotes a parallel from modern Fiji, which describes how the priest trembles, how distortions of his facial muscles follow, and twitching movements of his limbs, till the whole frame is violently convulsed, and it is recognized that the god is upon him and speaks through him; there is a shrill cry, "It is I! it is I!"; the priest's eyes roll in frenzy; his voice is unnatural, his face pale, his breathing depressed, and his appearance like a madman's, as he sweats and weeps.[1]

It is quite well recognized that these phenomena can be induced, but that does not affect the interpretation. To the ancient, as to the savage of to-day, the matter does not admit of doubt. The person possessed is conscious of the god; and there is no

---

[1] Jevons, "Intr. to History of Religion," 273; Williams, "Fiji and the Fijians," i. p. 224.

other obvious explanation; therefore that is the right one; the god enters the human being, and all that follows is natural and intelligible. The god therefore is real. Mystical vision gives the same results. The famous modern Bengali saint, Remakrishna Paramahamsa, in one trance saw and spoke with Jesus (for three days) and in another saw Kali dancing on the body of her husband Siva; therefore both gods were real, both religions were true, and, by a swift inference, all religions were true, and perhaps equally true. Prophecy gives the same results; where a prediction or a dream comes true, a god inspired or sent it; and Homer tells us how Zeus sent a lying dream to Agamemnon to spur him on to lead the Greeks to disaster. At Eleusis, Aristotle says, the participants in the mysteries were put into frames of mind and had feelings; and that of course proved the validity of what the priests said; those feelings were produced by the goddess; therefore the goddess was real, and men and women really had intercourse with her.

It will be noticed that in all these cases the presence of the god is proved by physical evidence, or rather is inferred from an explanation, or lack of explanation (which is the same thing) of physiological phenomena. Perhaps the case of prophecy is not the same; it is at least a little more complicated. The oracles long served as proof of the reality of the pagan gods. The absence of any moral element is the common weakness of this type of religious experience.

Plato had no high opinion of prophets and their art; and though he used Orphic terms, for the Orphists and their followers he had very shrewd criticism. In the "Timæus" (70, 72) his irony makes play with the mysterious nature of the prophetic gift. The authors of our being were charged by their Father to make the human race as good as they could; so they did something for our inferior parts too, and placed in the liver the seat of divination; "and herein is a proof that God has given the art of divination not to the wisdom, but to the foolishness of man; for no man in his wits attains prophetic truth and inspiration; but when he receives the inspired word, either his intelligence is enthralled by sleep, or he is demented by some distemper or possession. And he who would understand what he remembers to have been said, whether in a dream or when he was awake, by the prophetic and enthusiastic nature, or what he has seen, must first recover his wits. . . . Such is the nature and position of the liver."[1] Elsewhere Plato connects prophecy and lunacy (*mantikê* and *manikê*).[2] The poet, he says, is a light and winged and holy thing, but there is no invention in him till he has a god in him and his wits out of him.[3] If in the "Ion" Plato is laughing

---

[1] Jowett's translation.
[2] Plato, "Phædrus," 244.
[3] Plato, "Ion," 534 B.

gently at the artistic temperament, none the less the combination is to be noted, the god in possession and the mind no longer in the man.

In his very interesting tract on the "Cessation of Oracles," written about 100 A. D., Plutarch gives an account of how a shepherd, called Korêtas, came upon a jet or exhalation of some vapour near Delphi, and uttered words god-possessed (*enthousiodeis*), how people paid no attention, but were surprised to find that the words came true. "It is not to be wondered at, if while earth sends up many jets (*rheumata*), these are the only ones which bring the soul into an *enthusiastic* state, a state that can picture the future." Just as the eye is adapted to the light, so the body is constituted with regard to the prophetic spirit (*mantikon pneuma*). "The mantic jet and breath (*rheuma* and *pneuma*) is most divine and holy, and probably by heat and diffusion opens certain pores, or channels (*porous*), that can picture the future." That we are right in treating the *pneuma* as something like a natural gas exhaled by the earth, Plutarch's explanation of its occasional failure proves, when he suggests that, just as hot-water springs sometimes fail and reappear, and as the silver mines of Attica were exhausted, so heavy rainfalls and thunderbolts or earthquakes may shift these exhalations or extinguish them. A speaker in the dialogue wants to know what becomes of gods

THE HOLY SPIRIT

and dæmons if we resolve the prophetic gift "into breaths (*pneumata*) and vapours and exhalations."[1] Of course the answer is ready; there is a double cause, a divine agent and a physical means, and so forth; so that sacrifice does play a part in the obtaining of an oracle.

I quote this interesting passage, because it puts so vividly before us the confusion between an exhalation of breath—or gas, in our modern vocabulary—and spirit, between the material and the spiritual. One word covers both, *pneuma*, and the jarring is not felt, probably because it was the prevailing philosophic belief that all existence was material. Two and a half centuries after Plutarch, Augustine tells us what a struggle he had to get away from the notion that God was infinitely subtle matter.

To sum up, then, the world all around the Church believed in an infinite number of quasi-spiritual beings (if still somewhat material), gods and dæmons, who could possess the souls and bodies of men and women, and give them, sometimes prophetic speech, sometimes disease or madness, constantly change of personality; but in general it is not suggested that these beings are necessarily moral, or that the effects of their entering into men and women are really ethical. Plutarch does all he can to moralize

[1] Plutarch *de defectu oraculorum*, Sections 42, 40, 43, 46; lying between pp. 432 D and 435 A. In 437 C he speaks of variations, of the temple being filled with fragrance and *pneuma*.

his religion, but that was his own personal endeavour. Many dæmons were frankly immoral and evil, as he admits. The broad effects of this belief in possession by spirits were to stereotype the primitive traits in religion, to concentrate attention on ritual and the external, on the *taboo* instead of moral purity, and to emphasize the irrational as the highest expression of religion. Mystery became a synonym for esoteric knowledge, and feeling overbore thought and usurped its functions. Clarity was the enemy of piety, the intellect of the truest holiness.

II

As the Hebrews knew many of the same phenomena and shared at first the same beliefs, some repetition may be avoided. The prophets, the schools of the sons of the prophets, of which their oldest books speak, practised inspiration on lines still maintained by the Semitic dervish, as the story of Saul reminds us. That unhappy king, with his tendency to madness, was naturally amenable to the influence of the *nabi* or prophet, and lost himself among them; "the spirit of God came mightily upon him."[1] The abnormal psychical phenomena were the surest proof of the presence of the Spirit of God;[2] the king prophesying naked and lying naked

[1] 1 Samuel x. 10, xix. 20-24.
[2] Humphreys, "Holy Spirit," p. 41.

THE HOLY SPIRIT

on the ground a whole day and night was obviously inspired. We may compare the "parable" of a more professional prophet:[1]

> The oracle of Balaam, the son of Beor,
> The oracle of the man whose eye is closed,
> The oracle of him that heareth the words of God,
> Who seeth the vision of the Almighty,
> Fallen down and having the eyes uncovered.

Prophecy is associated with ecstasy and with possession; and at first, whether it is true or false, it is also associated with Jehovah. "The spirit of Jehovah had departed from Saul, and an evil spirit from Jehovah troubled (or terrified) him."[2] Jehovah sends "a lying spirit" to be in the mouth of Ahab's prophets and to deceive him.[3] Jeremiah fears that he himself may be the victim of the same fate.[4] The dream, too, is a regular instrument for the conveyance of God's will.

This is all very like what we find in the Greek world, in Fiji, in savage Africa. It was not at first that the prophets conceived of a God who would speak to a man when his wits were in him and he was awake. But the great prophets reached that point, and it differentiates them from the schools or droves of old-style prophets, whom perhaps we must not call impostors, but who certainly lent

[1] Numbers xxiv. 3, 15.
[2] 1 Samuel xvi. 14.
[3] 1 Kings xxii. 19-23.
[4] Jeremiah xx. 7; cf. p. 149.

themselves to imposture. The conception which a man has of God is normative for the rest of his thinking; and the high view of God held by the great prophets went with the sanity of their prophecy. God was to be reached by the whole man at his highest and best; and conversely, when the spirit of the Lord came on a man, with whatever excitation it came, it claimed the whole of him, intuition, insight, reflexion and reason.

How they would have defined "the spirit of the Lord," it might be difficult to guess; it is not a phrase for which men usually ask definition; in this region of thought and experience, we are conspicuously driven to metaphor. The "breath of the Lord" might be a more literal rendering, but it would not tell us anything further. "Influence," the vague, modern word, is also indefinite, till we know what is supposed to "flow in" from the one to the other. However, just as the heathen gods were believed to enter their devotees, so men at first believed the spirit of Jehovah to affect His adherents in mental disorder and eccentricity.[1] When the great prophets put forward another view of inspiration, one feature of the older belief remained and acquired a new significance; there was a personal contact between God and the man He "took," [2] closer, more intimate and more real, for it meant conference and com-

[1] To this day we are told that the Arabs regard the insane as the special wards of God and not to be harmed by man.
[2] Amos vii. 15.

THE HOLY SPIRIT

munion between God and man on the highest themes and in the highest way, and left no shame behind.[1] It is to be noted that while "the spirit of the Lord" is a regular phrase in the Old Testament, the combination "Holy Spirit" only occurs in two passages.[2]

One effect of the rise of Monotheism in the period after the Exile, was the growth of a feeling that God must not be brought too rudely into contact with the world of sense. The days were past when God would breathe into the nostrils of a creature His hands made, when He would walk in a garden with footsteps that could be heard. Intermediaries[3] were sought for the lowly work of creation; and between God and man stood His Wisdom, His Glory,[4] His Name,[5] and the Law.[6] For our purpose the Wisdom of God is of more significance, personalized, like some of these other conceptions, first by poetic feeling, and then by philosophic fancy. "Wisdom is a spirit that loves man."[7]

Wisdom is more mobile than any motion;
Yea, she pervadeth and penetrateth all things by reason of her pureness.
For she is a breath ($ἀτμίς$) of the power of God
And a clear effluence ($ἀπόρροια$) of the glory of the Almighty;

[1] *Cf.* 2 Samuel vi. 22.
[2] Psalm li. 11; Isaiah lxiii. 10, 11.
[3] See J. P. Peters' "Religion of the Hebrews," 392, 393.
[4] Tobit xiii. 14, xii. 15.
[5] Tobit xiii. 11, viii. 5.
[6] The law becomes the light that lightens every man, "Test. Levi," xiv. 4.
[7] Wisdom i. 6.

There can nothing defiled find entrance into her,
For she is an effulgence (ἀπαύγασμα) from everlasting light,
And an unspotted mirror of the working of God
And an image (εἰκών) of His goodness.
And she, though but one, hath power to do all things,
And remaining in herself reneweth all things;
And from generation to generation passing into holy souls,
She maketh them friends of God and prophets.
For nothing doth God love save him that dwelleth with wisdom.[1]

So writes the author of "The Wisdom of Solomon." Mr. Fairweather, on the writer's data, finds Wisdom in some midway position between an attribute of God, a poetic personification, and a divine personality subordinate to God; and as such a personality Wisdom, according to the judgment of another scholar, is clad with all the attributes of Deity. The alternatives seem to a prosaic mind, trained in Greek ways of thought, to be mutually exclusive; but in this sphere literalism is predestined failure to capture the idea. At another place the writer borrows the greatest of all Greek words, and calls Wisdom "thy almighty Logos" (xviii. 15)—an identification fruitful in theological thought; and in yet another place he asks, "Who knew Thy counsel, except Thou hadst given Wisdom, and sent Thy holy spirit (τὸ ἅγιόν σου πνεῦμα) from the highest?" (ix. 17). As the long passage already quoted attributes to Wisdom the making of prophets, it is an easy transition to that standard belief, which we find as an axiom

[1] Wisdom vii. 24 ff.

of general acceptance in the New Testament, that the Scriptures are the work of the Holy Spirit.

The Hebrews travelled a long way from the gross and crude conceptions with which they started, and developed an idea of divine relations with man, which, in spite of obvious confusions, proved of real value.

III

When we come to the New Testament, the first thing is to look at our authorities;[1] and, classifying them on the basis of their references to the Holy Spirit, we obtain a curious and new grouping of them. The Synoptic Gospels are generally and properly classed together, but in regard to the Holy Spirit Mark and Matthew are alike in the fewness of their allusions (apart from the birth, the baptism, and the temptation),[2] while Luke is in striking contrast. There are passages in Matthew where Dr. Denney[3] finds a colour from the language of a later day (vii. 22), but elsewhere that colour is remarkable by its absence, a guaranty of historicity (xvi. 18 ff., xviii. 15 f., passages dealing with the "church"). The trinitarian baptismal formula at the

[1] In what follows I draw a good deal from Dr. James Denney's article on the Holy Spirit in "The Dictionary of Christ and the Gospels"; references will be given briefly with his name and the page and column of that work.

[2] Mark six (one ref. to O.T.); Matthew eleven (with same ref. to O.T.).

[3] Denney, pp. 734 b, 735 a.

end, there is some reason for believing to be a revision after the Council of Nicæa, though this is disputed. Luke,[1] on the other hand, is greatly interested in the Spirit and finds a place for it at a number of points in the experience of Jesus—at the temptation, both where it begins and ends (iv. 1, 14); his rejoicing in the Spirit (x. 21); the substitution of the Spirit for the "good things" which God will give (xi. 13); and "the promise of my Father," viz. "power from high" (xxiv. 49); in the Acts the manifestations are naturally much more striking and numerous. Paul's writings abound in thoughts of the Holy Spirit, mentioned, it is said, one hundred and twenty times. The writer to the Hebrews in general is silent,[2] while the fourth gospel is written largely on the basis of the Spirit as the keynote of the new religion.

In the Gospels there is a very remarkable absence of the phenomena associated with the Spirit in the first century Church. That the contrast was felt by the early Christians is shown in their emphasis on Pentecost. The historian will feel a parallel between some of these manifestations in the Church and those noted in Greece and elsewhere, and described in the story of King Saul and in the Æneid. The nearest thing to them in the life of Jesus is the statement of Luke that "he rejoiced in the spirit," though here

[1] Denney, 735 a.
[2] Of the seven references to the Spirit in Hebrews, three refer to the Scriptures or the tabernacle.

THE HOLY SPIRIT

another translation is possible if not probable, and a single passage and a doubtful piece of translation are hardly warrant for bringing him into line with demonstrations which the greater prophets did without, which the Church soon outgrew, and which are not akin to his general mind and character.

Dr. Denney, a scholar who had a name for caution and for essential orthodoxy, has a paragraph on this matter, which with reserve and sanity puts the case admirably. "If, then, we try to sum up the oldest Evangelic representation, we can hardly say more than that the Holy Spirit is the Divine power which from his baptism onward wrought in Jesus, making him mighty in word and deed—a power the character of which is shown by the teaching and by the saving miracles of Jesus—a power to which the sanctity of God attached, so that it is Divine also in the ethical sense, and to blaspheme it is the last degree of sin—a power in which Jesus enabled his disciples in some extent to share, and which he promised would be with them in the emergencies of their mission—a power, however, which (contrary to what we might have anticipated), the Evangelist [Mark] does not bring into prominence at any of the crises or intense moments of Jesus' life. It takes nothing less than that life itself, from beginning to end, to show us what the Spirit means. If the last Evangelist tells us that the Spirit interprets Jesus, the inference from the first is that Jesus also interprets the Spirit, and that only from him can we know what it means."

IV

In the early Church we find ourselves in confusion, of which, it is well to remember that Paul says God is not the author (1 Cor. xiv. 33)—and this in a passage where he is speaking of spiritual manifestations. It is quite plain that the followers of Jesus in Jerusalem and in Corinth did not move on his plane of intellectual clarity. They grouped a great many of their experiences together and attributed them all to the Holy Spirit. First and most obvious were the psychopathic; speaking with tongues and speaking in ecstasy impressed them, as they did the heathen around them, and as they have since impressed Christians in England and America, and in the nineteenth century.[1] To us these things are evidence only of disturbance, to them they were proof of the presence of the Spirit. Prophecy, which Paul distinguishes from ecstatic speech, was as mysterious and as convincing; and there were converts who brought over from heathenism mystical ideas not found in the Synoptic Gospels and not very

[1] Once more let me refer to Mr. Davenport's most interesting book, "Primitive Traits in Religious Revivals" (Macmillan Co., New York). He gives a good many instances of such phenomena. John Wesley's "Journal" will also occur to readers, and the strange happenings in his early ministry in the neighbourhood of Bristol.

cognate with the teaching of Jesus. "The kingdom of God is not eating and drinking," said Paul (Romans xiv. 17), but men and women, trained in heathen circles to believe that with food a dæmon or a god might easily, and often did, enter the human system, took naturally another view of the Holy Spirit and its influence, and of the sacrament.

But if the early Christians shared so far the psychological views of their contemporaries, there were things associated by them with the Holy Spirit quite distinct from the psychopathic. Most important of all is conversion. The phenomena that accompany conversion and even conversion itself are, as we learnt from Dr. William James' famous book, not peculiarly Christian. Yet the conversion to a belief in Christ, with the moral changes which it inaugurates, with the uplifting conviction, the freedom (2 Cor. iii. 17), and the confidence in God (Rom. viii. 14), belonged to another order of things than the tongues and prophecies, and deserved the attention and the ascription it received. What else, they might well ask, could guarantee the eager sense of being the children of God (Rom. viii. 16)—of being free from the burdens of the law and (more wonderful) from all that is summed up as "the mind of the flesh" (Rom. viii. 6-9), from the degrading impulses, and from the haunting sense of condemnation (Rom. viii. 1, 30)—of being free in prayer, free in outlook—of being safe and assured against all the ills of this world, against assaults of "principalities and powers" here or hereafter, in the love of Christ—of victory beyond one's dreams? The eighth chapter of Romans is not a theoretical picture; it is the autobiography of one of the greatest and profoundest men in history, and it above all other writings tells the tale of the new life. If the early Christian grouped all this with tongues and the rest, we need not; and if we find an explanation for the glossolaly, we are bound to try to find one for the change that Paul experienced from death to life. The two groups of experiences do not stand together.

This indeed Paul saw. He speaks of the fruits of the Spirit as love, joy, peace, long-suffering, gentleness, goodness, faith, meekness, self-government (Gal. v. 22, 23); and among the gifts of the Spirit he reckons such things as the word of wisdom, the word of knowledge, faith, and the faculty of telling the difference between one spirit and another (1 Cor. xii. 8–11). All these are of one category, gifts that make the reality of life, without which men will not be really human. The list is not very Greek; it includes virtues and graces not much cultivated by the Greeks and rather forgotten by the Stoics themselves. But among them we must particularly notice the last-named. It was above all things needed in that early church. Paul surprises us by confessing that he himself "spoke with tongues" (I Cor. xiv. 18), and giving thanks for it; but he clearly prefers to speak intelligibly. Even if he does speak with tongues—tongues of men, if that is what they prove to be, or tongues of angels, which sounds like a quotation from somebody addicted to unintelligibility (1 Cor. xiii. 1)—love matters a great deal more; tongues will cease, love will abide (1 Cor. xiii. 8, 13). One of the tasks of love is to help other people, and to be intelligible to them especially on the greatest of themes; sanctified sense was what the Church needed, the gift of distinguishing between spirits. For it is plain that otherwise the Church would be swamped with foolery and blasphemy (1 Cor. xiv. 23, xii. 3).

When once then the noisier and more trivial manifestations are put in their place, whether they come from the Holy Spirit or some other spirit or are, as we might say, pathological, there remains the task of explaining the very great new gifts of the Church. With the language of the Old Testament written in the very hearts of Paul and the other Christian Jews, certain modes of speech were inevitable. Take the language of Isaiah, and read it with the commentary afforded by "The Wisdom of Solomon" (a book very familiar to Paul), and the ascription of the new life to the Spirit of God cannot be resisted. There was fluctuation as to the right way of naming it. Luke, in some texts, calls it "the spirit of Jesus" (Acts xvi. 7); and Paul at times identifies the Spirit and the Lord (2 Cor. iii. 17, 18); he urges now that "the spirit of God dwells in you" (1 Cor. iii. 16), now that "Jesus Christ is in you" (2 Cor. xiii. 5); he prays that his friends may be "strengthened with might by God's spirit in the inner man" and in the next sentence that "Christ may dwell in their hearts by faith" (Eph. iii. 16, 17), and then immediately equates knowing the love of Christ, and being filled with all the fulness of God (Eph. iii. 19).

Greek theories of the world and of life pointed the same way. The Stoic never tired of telling men that they were fragments of God, particles of divine breath; and this was not mere rhetoric, but part of a thought-out system. Through all nature went a *Logos*—a word or principle, intellectual, assimilable by the mind; it was *spermatikos,* life-giving, the germinal secret of all life, and it was in man. Seneca wrote to Lucilius that there is "a holy spirit dwelling within us—our guardian. . . . None is good without God."[1] It is true that the same claim might be made—would be made—by the Stoic for every animate creature and inanimate. The Stoic and the Christian conceptions of the Holy Spirit were really quite different; the one relates it to all life, the lowest included, and involves it in the meanest and the wickedest actions;[2] the other finds the highest life alone in the Spirit and not elsewhere.

[1] Seneca, "Ep." 41, 1, 2.
[2] This was pointed out by Plutarch in his tracts criticising the Stoics, and by Clement of Alexandria; "Conflict of Religions," p. 97.

THE HOLY SPIRIT

There is a gap between Greek and Hebrew here; and the Greek will say that the Christian view is not free from vagueness, there is something undefined about it.

To this there is a twofold reply. There is a great deal that is undefined about the early Christian doctrine of the Spirit; "it doth not yet appear what we shall be" (1 John iii. 2); and in Paul's words but "God has given the earnest of the spirit in our hearts" (2 Cor. i. 22), the "earnest of our inheritance" (Eph. i. 14), while the fourth gospel attributes to Jesus himself the promise that the Spirit is to "guide you into all truth" (or "in all truth," John xvi. 13). How can men be precise till they have the whole of the facts before them? But, meanwhile, the second line of reply is stronger. The people who use this language are trying to translate into words equal to conveying their meaning a new experience that eclipses everything they have known. If a man is "born again," is "a new creation," if he has repeated in everyday life the mystical experience of Paul, and lives in the vision of things unspeakable (2 Cor. xii. 4), in joy unspeakable and glorified (1 Peter i. 8), how is he to express or account for what he only realizes with surprise and a constant sense of more beyond? Is it of God this new life? There are the splendid crop of new virtues, the manhood, the power, the other obvious signs of development and *aretê;* if it is not God Who ministers them to man, where do they come from? But if after all God is coming into a man, as they used to believe that dæmons did, and is expelling the dæmons and their products, and filling a man with Himself, how is it to be expressed? Paul is like a man in love, too sure and too happy to analyse or define; more tongues than the "glossolalies" will pass away, vocabularies wear out and definitions grow old, but "who shall separate us from the love of Christ?" (Rom. viii. 35). Whether this is a proper reply or not, in our judgment, may perhaps depend on whether we put experience or definition first. Both are good. The early Christian, when asked for an explanation, said "God"; and if it was not clear how the great and ultimate God could come into a man, there was the great religious speech of the Hebrews available. God, Christ, the Spirit—which did he say? Well, all of them, any of them; it was the same thing, unspeakable.

V

It is a long way from this point of view to the so-called Athanasian Creed, with its language definite as a philosopher's and precise as a lawyer's, and a menace in every syllable. Yet we can see how that distance was traversed, and we shall remember that no definition is necessarily final, that menace is not the language of philosophy or of the Gospel. If Athanasius might champion a view of Christ *contra mundum,* we have at least the same right to cross-examine him on his grounds of belief. It is not a new discovery that the Christology of the New Testament is not Athanasian. The Athanasian Trinity may indeed be a true and necessary outcome of the premises yielded by the experience described in the New Testament; it may prove that there is ultimately no true philosophy of the universe but on the lines indicated in that creed; and if that be the case, whether we like it or not, some fundamental loss will be involved in a man's rejection of the real interpretation of God.

Meanwhile, however, the creed, as it stands, is in a foreign tongue, doubly or trebly foreign. A philosophic training is needed if we are to understand the Greek of Athanasius; and his Greek is at once old and not old enough; he is thinking in the categories of an age of tradition, using his terms with precision and clearness, but perhaps with more precision and clearness than a greater or more original thinker would manage or allow. All our categories, all our modes of thought, our preconceptions are changed; it is not necessary to say that they are inevitably sounder than those of Athanasius; that is the language of extreme youth in every period; but we think on different lines, and are really more at home with Plato than with Athanasius' contemporaries who called themselves the New Platonists. Then the language of Athanasius is translated into Latin, and that not the Latin we know best; and from Latin long ago, as much by transliteration as by translation, it reached English; and English has changed a good deal since those days. What are we to say to a creed, distant by so many removes from the language we use and the thoughts we think?

We have to remember that behind the theory of the Church lies experience, and another man's theory is not of much value to me without his experience. What is it that Athanasius, or the Church is trying to convey to us? That is one question, and a more urgent one is: What is the experience, what are the vital facts, that lie behind that language?

From one point of view the theory of the early Church on the Holy Ghost is very mechanical. A cup cannot simultaneously be full of (let us say) ink and of coffee; if you want to fill it with coffee, you must pour out the ink, and *vice versa*. Here is a man full of sin (no mistake about that); to make him full of righteousness, you must get out of him the dæmon that makes him bad, but you must not leave him empty, he must be spatially filled with another spirit, the spirit that produces righteousness. The laws of space and matter forbid both spirits being there together. The ancient attribution of material substance to what they called spirit had its part in shaping their doctrine of the Holy Spirit. Some even held that in some way the Holy Spirit

THE HOLY SPIRIT

was actually conveyed materially to the baptized by the water of baptism. The oddness of their doctrine of these alternative spirits is given by their materialism; but beside the oddness, there is truth. A parable of Jesus suggests that a man cannot safely remain empty;[1] positive active good is the only way to get rid of evil—the interest of the man must be put actively on to something new and good. We hold, and we find evidence for it in the teaching of Jesus, that the evil in a man is not the intrusion of an alien dæmon, but an expression of something that is (at any rate for the time) himself. Space and matter are not involved; but there must be a change of interest and attention. As Seeley said, no virtue is safe that is not enthusiastic; and if his adjective, natural and instinctive, recalls to us in this connexion its ancient meaning, it is still true—perhaps we shall say, truer.

The mechanical look, given by their materialism to their psychology, is not its most important feature. There are few thoughts so often or so beautifully emphasized by Plato as his belief that man is not an earthly but a heavenly plant,[2] born to be on terms of intimacy with God and to become like God,[3] that there is an essential aptitude between God and

[1] Luke xi. 24-26.
[2] "Timæus," 90 A; on the parallels between Plato and the N.T. on this point, see Adam's "Religious Teachers of Greece," 436-7.
[3] "Theætetus," 176 B.

man, and that the real norm of human life, as of all else, is God.[1] This is the fundamental belief underlying all religion—that relation between God and man is inevitable. The kinship in mind and ideas between God and man is Plato's contribution. How Jesus brought this kinship, re-inforced and heightened every way, into the hearts of men, the Gospels tell us; and the Christian community expressed it in one aspect in this doctrine of the Holy Spirit, in another in that of the Incarnation.

It is hard to imagine a stronger ground for believing a doctrine true than the visible transformation by it of character on a large scale, similarly over great areas and long periods, and among peoples of the most different racial and intellectual antecedents. What impressed the early Christian will still impress anyone candid enough to attend to it. The real struggle at Nicæa was over the Son, not over the Spirit. To-day the doctrine of the Holy Spirit suffers from its schematic precision, and from all the intellectual play that has been made by theologians with the number Three. Probably if it were again to formulate, it would take some different shape. But, important as adequate expression is for an idea, the form is not the supreme thing, but the fact which we are trying to express; and, if that relation between God and man, which the Church taught in its doctrine of the Holy Spirit, be not true, it is hard

[1] "Laws," 716.

THE HOLY SPIRIT

to see how religion can endure. But man has never believed that anything real is unintelligible; and the greatest venture he has made has been to assume that he can understand God. Jesus' whole life was given to demonstrating it, and history shows that the venture has been justified.

X

THE STATUE OF THE GOOD SHEPHERD

This story is a page out of the history of the Christian Church, or, to be strictly accurate, it is more like a page of a scrap-book. The scraps joined together here are all genuine, if what holds them together is conjecture. There was a statue made of the Good Shepherd or a wall-carving, and fairly early; perhaps not first in North Africa. But in any case it was made. The authentic first example of it may very well have perished; none the less, at or about the period with which we are dealing, a man had the conception, which, under his own hand and tool, or under the hand and tool of another commissioned by him, took the form which established the type. "A man of sense," says Plato, in the "Phædo," speaking of one of his myths, "ought not to say, nor will I be too confident, that the description which I have given . . . is exactly true. But I do say that . . . he may venture to think that something of the kind is true."[1] The scraps joined together come mostly from Tertullian; some come from his contemporary, Clement of Alexandria, and

[1] Plato, "Phædo," 114.

STATUE OF THE GOOD SHEPHERD 175

from other early Christian writers. The function of art, as Longinus says,[1] is to seize the vital elements and combine them so that the product lives. It is at least a high ideal to set before oneself.

There was, then—or let there have been—a sculptor in North Africa, not a great artist, no Michael Angelo, but something like those who to-day in England have their shops within a hundred yards of every considerable cemetery, who make conventional angels kneeling in prayer or hovering over a strong marble support, crosses, urns and broken columns and the like. In India they are still making gods, and doing it to pattern; holy men of old, we are told, invented the designs and they are still kept, and the first thing the sculptor has to do to make an idol is to get out his pattern. The man was rather the artisan than the artist, but this is not to say that he had no turn for his trade. Like Lucian the satirist, he may have been put in an uncle's shop, because as a schoolboy he would scrape the wax from the wax-tablet that served him for a slate at school, and mould it into figures; but unlike Lucian, who ran away when his uncle grew angry at a clumsy breakage, this man who had no turn for books and literature stuck to his trade.

Æsop's fables give us as good a picture of him as we need. The god Hermes or Mercury, he tells us, became a little self-conscious, and wanted to know

[1] See p. 264.

how men thought of him, what value for instance as compared with the other gods they set upon him. He dropped down to earth and went in disguise through a city till he found a sculptor. Through the open side of the shop he saw a number of gods standing there, and one of them was himself. So the god went in to see the sculptor, and, being the god of thieves and of shrewd people generally, he did not begin with the question he wished answered. He strolled about the shop and looked at the statues, and by and by asked the price of Jupiter. So much, said the sculptor. "Ah! and Juno over there, how much is she?" Such and such a price. "And Hermes?" "Look here!" said the sculptor, "if you will buy Jupiter and Juno, I'll throw Mercury in." And Æsop draws a moral which need not detain us. That was the kind of sculptor; given the marble and the pattern, he could repeat a piece indefinitely, and much on the same level, each copy about as good as the one before it.

He was a man of the people (*de vestris sumus*), a decent, kindly sort of man, judged by the common standards, which would not be too high. Living in a heathen town he took his pleasures as they came, the pleasures of heathen mankind of that day, in what men would have called moderation, but hardly "according to Christ" in Paul's phrase; but that was not to be expected. That he was not better than his neighbours he readily admitted; but he thought he was not much worse; and he jogged on through life, liking it and getting on very well, never aiming very high and remaining on the whole a little commonplace perhaps; but so do many people. Like everybody else he made a joke now and then, not very clever jokes perhaps; but nobody admits being destitute of a sense of humour; everybody has it; and like other people he would repeat his jokes.

After a while he came to know some Christian people, or some of his friends turned Christian, and this enlarged his range of humour, much to his satisfaction. He got several new jokes out of it, fairly obvious ones, but none the worse for that. It is not every pleasantry that will keep for seventeen hundred years, so perhaps they were not then so tedious as they may have become. He chaffed his friends on their change of belief and conduct, dealing first, as was natural, with the superficial. He made game of them and they took it good-temperedly. Sometimes they argued sensibly with him, and he grew flippant; sometimes they returned his fire with quips original or borrowed.

They kept none of the usual festivals, he noticed, they never put lighted lamps at their doors,[1] never wore garlands; and he told them, "It's a poor heart that never rejoices. Why do you never enjoy life, never even wear a garland? It is bad for trade,

[1] Tertullian, "Apology," 35; "Idolatry," 15; cf. "de corona militis," 7, 10.

too." The retort came: "No, I don't buy garlands for my head, but what difference does it make to the gardeners how I use flowers? I like them best when they are free and unbound and trailing everywhere. Even if they are done up in garlands, I smell with my nose, not with my hair;[1] I can't see them if I am crowned with them, and I am told that damp flowers round the head are bad for the brain."[2] "What about incense?" "No, we don't buy incense." "There you are!" "The money for that all goes to Arabia and abroad." "Oh!" "But do be sensible! How can we be bad for trade, when we live in the same way as everybody else; we aren't Brahmins or Indian sages who lived naked in the woods and fly from mankind. We go to the baths and the butchers as you do; we have to get everything in the market just as we used, and go to the same shops and inns and fairs.[3] Of course there are some trades we don't patronize, as you know very well—the soothsayers and astrologers don't get our money; nor the magicians and poisoners, nor the bullies and other dirty fellows."[4] Then the conversation stopped.

Next time they met, the sculptor took a more serious line. "If you aren't careful, you may have to stand before the judgment-seat of the pro-consul

[1] Tertullian, "Apology," 42.
[2] Clement Alex., "Pædagogus," ii. 70.
[3] Tertullian, "Apology," 42.
[4] Tertullian, "Apology," 43.

STATUE OF THE GOOD SHEPHERD 179

one of these days." "And one of these days," rejoined his friend, more gravely still, "you *will* have to stand before the judgment-seat of Christ."

Again, they encountered in a quiet street, and his greeting, not loud enough for passers-by to hear, if there were any, was the common anti-Christian cry: "Away with the atheists!" "Whom do you mean?" "You, of course; you don't worship the gods." "But are you sure they are gods?" "Well, we reckon them gods; they are gods for us." [1] "For you? Then who is it robs their temples?—it is not we! Gods for you! and look how you go and see them burlesqued on the stage—you told us about it not so long ago.[2] And look at the rubbish you offer them in sacrifice! Why, the other day a lot of your gods were being sold by auction! Look in your shop and see what the spiders think of your gods!" [3] "Never mind the spiders! It is our piety to the gods that made the Roman Empire what it is; the gods built it up for us!" "What? Jupiter who was buried in Crete, do you mean? [4]—a foreign god, and dead and buried at that? Or—try a really Roman god! do you mean Sterculus [the dung-god]?" [5] The Christian paused, and then began again: "How many emperors do you recognize?" "One, of

---
[1] Tertullian, "Apology," 13.
[2] Tertullian, "Apology," 15.
[3] Tertullian, "Apology," 14; 13; 12.
[4] Tertullian, "Apology," 25.
[5] Tertullian, "Apology," 25.

course." "Not more?" "Good God, no! I don't want a trial for treason!" "Stop a minute! what do you mean when you say 'Good God!' like that?" "Oh! it's just an expression." "An expression of what?" "I don't know What are you getting at?" "Don't you see? When you speak naturally you only recognize *one God! 'Good God'* you say, and 'God sees,' and 'I leave it to God.' You really *know*—your soul knows—that there is only *one* God; your soul is Christian, if you're not!"[1] "I never thought of that." "No, of course you didn't; you haven't thought much about it at all." "Well, perhaps I haven't; I'm just an ordinary man. But, I say, what made you ask if I recognized more emperors than one?" "Oh! just this. If you did, it wouldn't mean there were more emperors than one; but the one emperor would let you know how many emperors there are, if he got to hear of it." "By Jove! he would." "And supposing there's only one God, what will He say to you, if you tell him what you told me, 'We reckon the others gods; they are gods for us'?" The sculptor held his tongue; then he laughed and said: "It might be pretty awkward. Well! good-bye." He went off to his shop, and the first thing he noticed was a new spider-web hanging between Jupiter and Mercury. "Well!" he ejaculated, "if that isn't what he said just now? It's odd!" And perhaps he thought a little.

[1] Tertullian, "Apology," 17.

STATUE OF THE GOOD SHEPHERD

A festival came round; and returning from it, merry and crowned, he met one of his dismal Christian friends and rallied him: "All gloom and no garlands again!" "You don't seem to realize that my crown may be coming in the next world.[1] Besides, you don't see what you are doing; you are always bothering us to wear crowns of flowers, but what you gave our Master was a crown of thorns."[2] "A crown of thorns? I never heard of that!" "No!" said the Christian, "there are quite a lot of things you never heard of. You prefer *not* to know what we say. You are inquisitive about everything else in the world; you are always wanting to know; but when it comes to Christianity, you aren't inquisitive, you don't want to know![3] It's much easier to make fun of things you don't understand and don't know. Why don't you come to one of our meetings and know what we really mean and what we believe? Afraid of the police and the spies?" That the sculptor repudiated; he was not afraid of anything. "Not afraid of hearing what we say?" "No!" "Then come and hear it."

At last they prevailed on him to come on a Sunday.[4] They brought him by a roundabout way and back streets into an upper room. He had been

---
[1] Tertullian, "De Corona Militis," 15.
[2] *Ibid.*, 14; Clement Alex., "Pædagogus," ii. 73.
[3] Tertullian, "ad Nationes," i. 1.
[4] Sunday: Justin Martyr, "Apology," 67, from which this description of the meeting is taken.

in temples often, at festivals, on ordinary occasions, sometimes too delivering gods that had been ordered or doing repairs. But he had never seen any temple like this; there was no god, no altar, and no very obvious priest; and, the strangest thing of all, there was no ritual worth talking about, and everything was intelligible, at least so far as words went. Passages were read at some length from the commentaries or Memoirs of the Apostles, as they called them to him, though sometimes they called them Gospels; and from the writings of the Jewish prophets. He was not scholar enough to realize how bad, how illiterate the Latin was;[1] but he found the prophets not very lucid; the Gospels were clearer for ordinary people. When the reading was done, someone rose and in a speech urged all present to follow the great example set to them in these books. Then all stood and prayer was made to Christ, just as prayer was made in the temples of the gods,[2] and they sang. They ended their prayers with a foreign word which he did not know, *Amen*; one or two substituted *Alleluia*.[3] Money was collected, for the poor and sick apparently. Altogether it was an odd ritual, and a little dull; it lacked pomp and spectacle, and made a heavier demand on attention and intelligence than ordinary temple cere-

[1] *Cf.* Arnobius, i. 58, 59; and Augustine, "Confessions."
[2] Pliny's letter to Trajan on Christian worship, "Epp." x. 96, 7.
[3] Tertullian, "de Oratione," 27.

STATUE OF THE GOOD SHEPHERD 183

monies. Still he had been interested in the Memoirs, and was struck with the earnestness of the speakers and with the atmosphere of friendship.

After some weeks he went again, and by and by became a not infrequent attender. He grew more interested in the books and in the extraordinary correspondence between the Gospels and the Prophets. Could the story really have been all foretold? Were the prophecies genuine? On that, they told him, he could ask the Jews. Some of the things preached were quite silly—"all that about dead men rising"; he said, "of course dead men don't rise; you know that as well as I." When they persisted; "Well!" he said, "you don't make it true by talking about it. If talk made things true, we should have to believe all that the religious imposters tell us, and the miracle-mongers in the market-place.[1] It doesn't happen." "How do you know it didn't happen?" "A question like that isn't necessary." By and by he heard more about the judgment-seat of Christ, and realized what they had meant by it. It was not a pleasant theme; it was uncomfortable—all that talk about the Judge's left hand; still the Christians believed it, and either that or something else affected their lives. For it was quite clear they were decent honest people, intensely kind and eager to help the

[1] See Lucian's "Lover of Lies," full of such people and their tales; and Celsus, quoted by Origen, "contra Celsum," i. 68, miracles for coppers; and Marcus Aurelius, i. 6.

wretched;[1] and one man, whom he saw among them, he recognized as formerly a professional thief, though he was learning a trade now. There were slaves too, on whom nobody looked down, which surprised him a good deal at first, but he came to know them, and found they were not like ordinary slaves—not so bitter or so small-minded, but happy and honest, and not unmanly.

Still, when he really pulled himself together, he saw that the whole fabric of their talk was rotten. God's love was not a very sound idea; it was sentimental; and one day he came across a parody of the Incarnation story, which amused him very much, and which he fired off at his friends. He had heard how somebody, who had written a book,[2] had compared Christians to frogs sitting round their pond, and croaking out to one another a story of God becoming one of them because He loved them;— "really, when you think of it, from the gods' point of view, away up beyond the air, there can't be much difference between frogs and men." Yes, the frogs croaked away and told how God meant to save the frogs who believed—and even the tadpoles— when He came and burnt up the rest of the world with fire, like a clumsy cook. It was really a very good take-off of what the Christians told him.

---

[1] I Clement Rom. ii. 2.
[2] The comparison comes from Celsus' "True Word," written in 176 A.D. against the Christians. *Cf.* Origen, "contra Celsum," iii. 71.

So he did not seem very likely to become a convert, though he was not unfriendly. "He remains interested," one Christian would say to another, "but only fitfully; and he does not show any signs of joining us—unless that he argues where he used to laugh. He was wanting to know whether we would take him if he accepted Jesus and kept the rest of the gods; and now this silly parody about the frogs comes up, whenever we talk with him."

By and by a great day came. There were going to be beasts shows, gladiator shows, in the amphitheatre. The fascination of them we learn from the tale of the student in St. Augustine's *Confessions*. The sculptor liked them—at least, he had always liked them and he resolved to go. His Christian friends, of course, would not go; but he was not a Christian, and he went and got a good seat from which he could see everything. The great place quickly filled up with crowds of people in high expectation. He had not been there very long before he realized there was some special excitement; there was trouble on foot, he soon saw; Christian trouble. The cry rose and was taken up all round: "Away with the atheists!" and then: "The Christians to the lions!" The whole place was seething with excitement and confused shouting, that concentrated again and again in these cries.

All sorts of things surged through the sculptor's mind. He would like to get out, but that was impossible now, and it might lead to suspicions. "Who could have denounced them? Was there a spy there last Sunday night? That Jew?[1] I wonder if he saw me!" The man's heart sank; and then he thought of his friends: "I wonder whom they have got! O God!" And he lapsed into that natural monotheism of the soul of which they had spoken to him. The shouting grew in volume; hard faces fired with fury and rage.[2] The man next him looked at him: "What's the matter?" The sculptor concealed his alarm, and lied hurriedly: "I don't feel well." "That's a pity," said the man, and fell to shouting *Christianos ad leones*[3] and forgot him.

His seat commanded the entrance to the arena, and he saw the gate thrown open. Everybody looked at once, leaping on the seats and all shouting more than ever. He must see, so he, too, mounted his seat, in time to see one—two—three—four men dragged in—then two women—another man, all of them stripped to the skin. They were led to the centre of the arena and tied to stakes there. The women had both recently had babies, one of them in prison; and for some curious reason the mob insisted on their being clothed; something was flung over them, and then the show began in earnest. The

---

[1] Tertullian, "Apol.," 7; "Scorpiace," 10.
[2] Tertullian, "de Spectaculis," 15, 16.
[3] On this cry and its variations, *cf.* Tertullian, "Apology," 40; "de Resurrectione Carnis," 22; "de Spect.," 27.

STATUE OF THE GOOD SHEPHERD 187

sculptor knew them both; one of them he had heard tell her visions at the Christian meeting, a gentle lady—and it came to this! One of the men seemed to be looking in his direction; did they recognize him? Could they think he had sold them?—horrible thought! He could not tell them he was loyal— could not help them—could not get away—could not take his eyes off them. A savage cow was let loose on them and tossed both women; and every cruel passion in human nature released itself in delight and yelling. Then shouts for a lion. From the entrance he saw a leopard come out, prodded from behind, startled by the howling crowd. Catlike, when it saw the naked victims in front, it lay flat on the ground and crept nearer. The silence grew tense, everybody watched and held his breath.[1] Suddenly the beast made a big spring, it leapt on the back of Saturus and ripped it open. The man was drenched with his own blood. Some witty spectator called out: "Washed and saved," and in a moment the thousands were shouting it at the bleeding man —*Salvum lotum! salvum lotum!* The whole story is in Tertullian's *Acts of the Martyrdom of Felicitas and Perpetua*. The sculptor saw it all; at last it was over, and he got out of the amphitheatre, resolved never to enter it again. He reached home somehow, tingling and disturbed. He sat down in front of one of his idols; he could not work, he could not

[1] On this interval of tension, *cf*. Tertullian, "de Pudicitia," 22.

think; he broke down and wept. The week passed in a storm of misery and unrest.

On the Sunday night he sought out what was left of the Christian meeting. It was smaller than before, smaller by more gaps than the martyrs would have filled. One or two looked at him doubtfully, and at last the presiding member asked him why he had come. He said: "I want to be baptized." "But why?" "Because nobody could die like that unless he knew he was right." They soon were clear that he had come over to them in earnest, that the blood of the martyrs was indeed the seed of the church;[1] but they deferred his baptism till he should learn more of the faith he was to profess. He became a catechumen.

At last, after weeks of waiting and learning, his catechumenate was ended, and on Easter day, clad in white, he received his baptism; and, as with all who receive it in adult life, it meant a great deal to him. He formally renounced the devil, his pomp and his angels, and professed publicly his faith, using a formula already taught him; he was then immersed three times in the name of the Father, the Son, and the Holy Spirit. As he came from the baptistery (*lavacrum*), they gave him a mixture of milk and honey; they anointed him, and laid their hands on his head, inviting the Holy Spirit in bene-

[1] Tertullian, "Apology," 50; "Ad Scapulam," 5.

STATUE OF THE GOOD SHEPHERD 189

diction.[1] Afterwards he was admitted to the Communion of the Lord's Supper. He went home with a joy he had never known before; he belonged to Christ; his sins were forgiven, a new life lay before him and immortality beyond it. He was wonderfully happy,[2] and sang Christian hymns as he carved his statues. He was a new man.

Here, perhaps, the pen should be laid down; for what follows, I am told, is anti-climax. But so is most of life. The novelist, for intsance, reaches his climax in his last pages and leaves his readers to infer the rest; all that follows the union of lovers must be dull, progressively dull. Life would be different if managed on that plan, certainly shorter; and happily all Christians were not martyred immediately after their baptism. Our sculptor lived on, and, if our reconstruction of his story is right, it was in the years of anti-climax and routine that he did his work. Felicitas and Perpetua gave their great testimony in the arena; he gave his in his shop. He might have repeated theirs; perhaps he did; perhaps he did re-enter the amphitheatre once more; but his chief work was in the shop, and it came about somehow so.

A stranger came to the Christian meeting—a man you would know again if you saw him once, a crea-

[1] Tertullian, "de Baptismo," 7, 8; "de Corona Militis," 2; see H. M. Gwatkin, "Church History," vol. i. p. 251.
[2] Clement Alex., "Pædagogus," i. 22.

ture of imagination, all on fire, a master of telling words, with flashing eyes, keen face, and sensitive lips.[1] He preached on Idolatry—on the real meaning of its renunciation in baptism; how insidious it is—not only an affair of definitely worshipping idols, but of doing anything which brings honour to the evil spirits represented by idols, or makes their worship effective or attractive, or recognizes them in any way whatever. "No art, no profession, no trade, which plays a part in the equipment or the formation of idols can lack the accusation of idolatry."[2] "You," cried the speaker, flashing out an indignant finger, "are a teacher; it is your business to train boys in literature; yes, to drill them in the names and pedigrees and legends of false gods; you keep their festivals as holidays, you dedicate the boy's first school fee to Minerva; on the birthday of every idol you decorate the school with flowers—you who renounced the devil, his pomp and his angels."[3] "And you," he wheeled round and the accusing finger pointed to another, "you are a painter, you press the gold leaf, you gild the temple of Satan; the plasterer, the carpenter, the mason, all lend their trades to the shrine."[4] "You," and the finger seemed to the sculptor to point directly

---

[1] The reader may have wondered why the sculptor never met Tertullian before, if they both knew Perpetua. Some of the scraps rearranged on the page may want a little more sorting.
[2] Tertullian, "Idolatry," 11.
[3] *Ibid.*, 10. [4] *Ibid.*, 11.

at himself, as the bow drawn at a venture drove the arrow home—"you are a sculptor! So from your idols you come to the church, from the shop of the enemy to the house of God, you lift up to God the Father hands that are mothers of idols, touch the body of the Lord with those hands, that outside give bodies to devils. Yes, and those hands give to others what they have defiled! The Jews once laid hostile hands on Christ, and yours every day do it to his body. Look well to it, whether he meant this too, when he said, 'If thy hand offend thee, cut it off!'"[1]

This was bad enough with the painful thoughts it waked of inconsistency, of apostasy and ingratitude. But the speaker was not done; he went on and tore to shreds every plea of defence. "I have no other way to live!" "You should have thought of that before; you have renounced the devil and his angels. The builder should count the cost, lest, after he has begun, he blush to find all spent." "I shall be in need!" "But the Lord calls the needy happy." "I shall have no food." "He said, 'Think not of food,' and as for clothing he pointed to the lilies." "But provision must be made for my children and posterity." "No man putting his hand to the plough and looking back is fit for work." "But I have a contract." "No man can serve two masters." "I have no means to live!" "Faith fears no famine.

[1] Tertullian, "Idolatry," 7.

What is hard with man is easy with God." [1] "But I sha'n't be able to live." *"Must* you live? I don't see the necessity. There are no *musts* where God is concerned." "Everybody does it; it is custom!" "Our Lord Jesus Christ called himself not custom but Truth." [2] And back he swung once more to the baptismal promise to renounce the devil, his pomps and his angels. "Can you really have renounced with the tongue, what you confess with the hand?" [3]

It is not easy for people who live in a land long Christian to realize how intricately religion is woven into life, but in every heathen land to-day questions of conscience arise at every turn for the Christian convert. If Chinese law requires, as it does, some act of veneration from every schoolboy to the picture of Confucius hung in the schoolroom, is that a token of mere respect or does it imply worship? Is Confucius a man or a god? Which does the law mean, and which do you mean? In India, I came to the conclusion that I had myself been guilty of what Tertullian, and others not so strict, would call idolatry—more than once. It is a common courtesy to give a visitor a garland; visiting temples with a government official in a native state, I accepted garlands, which were taken off the idol. I meant to be courteous, merely; I am no worshipper of the

[1] Tertullian, "Idolatry," 12.
[2] Tertullian, "De Virginibus Velandis," 1.
[3] "De Idololatria," 6.

Nandi; but it was arguable that I recognized the *Nandi* by accepting his garland. Probably, though not certainly, in the case of a European the act would not be strictly construed as recognition; but for a new convert "with conscience of the idol," it might be very different. Again, I once attended a performance of *Sakuntalam,* Kalidasa's famous play, in a missionary college, and, in my ignorance of Sanskrit, let my attention wander till I noticed a picture of the goddess *Sarasvati* set on a chair on the stage, and in front of it a plate with bananas and broken cocoanut. Later on, I realized more fully what it meant. It had a close analogy with the *stips* which Tertullian denounces as given to Minerva. *Uno colit asse Minervam,* says the Latin poet; what does *colit* mean? A Chinese reckoned some 170 trades as tinged with idolatry.

The sculptor went home in trouble. It *was* just. He had been untrue to his baptismal vow; he had been making his living off the devil and his angels, by carving their images. His tongue had sung hymns to Christ, while his hand worshipped the devil by making him. With a sigh—it was the hidden artist in the artisan that sighed—he turned his statues face to the wall; he was done with them for ever; and certain of his tools he laid aside. Tertullian had dropped a hint, a practical hint; and he took it. "The plasterer can mend roofs as well as daub temples; the painter, the marble-mason, the bronze-worker have other things they can do. How much sooner can he who carves a Mars out of a lime tree fasten together a chest! No art but is either mother or kin of another art. If the wages are smaller, they come oftener. To gild shoes and slippers is daily work; not so to gild Mercury and Serapis. Luxury and ostentation have more votaries than superstition." [1] We need not discuss the lawfulness of ministry to luxury; our poor hero was not gilder or shoemaker; but he could carve stones; and if it is luxury to have designs, friezes, ornaments about one's house, it is not so ostentatious as to wear gilded slippers. At any rate it was a loophole. Tertullian had not recognized how dull the change might be from sculptor to marble-mason; but if Christ preferred it, that was enough. So to the building trade he turned, and squared stones for them—square stones, flat stones, flat stones and square stones—an eternal monotony of right angles and straight lines—never the shoulders of Venus or the head of Apollo rising from the block with their splendid curves. Even a fifth-rate artist loves his art; and the sculptor gave it up. No more curves—at best, poor pomegranates in a row, or a long stiff garland of flowers; never the free glad touch of his art again. What a life! but it was better.

At last the thought came to him: Why not a

[1] "De Idololatria," 8.

statue of Christ Himself? It had never been done; there was no model, and he was of no use without a pattern; originality had never been his trade. Christians had used little devices in the flat.[1] The oldest and commonest was the anchor, an emblem of salvation, and not to be drawn without a cross. The cross itself they did not carve; it was still a symbol of shame and it attracted attention and derision, sometimes mutilation. The crucifix came late into Church use, not till after the victory of the Church; it was early used in parody by enemy and blasphemer. A cross made of four gammas was used, and so was the monogram of the initials of Jesus Christ ☧, a device also used by pagans with another meaning (*chrysos*, gold). The fish too is a very ancient symbol of Christ, because the Greek letters of it made an acrostic (ΙΧΘΥΣ)—Jesus Christ, God's Son, Saviour; just as Verdi became popular in the days of Italy's struggle for union, and had his name written up everywhere, because it had an acrostic value—Vittorio Emmanuele Re D'Italia. The fish and the composer's name were quite innocent things to carve and write up; they only spoke to those who understood. So well established was the fish, that Tertullian, in speaking of baptism, says: "We little fishes also, like our ΙΧΘΥΣ, Jesus Christ, are born in the water, and are only

[1] *Cf.* Marucchi, "Christian Epigraphy" (Eng. tr.), p. 59.

saved by remaining in the water." [1] Thus two little fishes are drawn moving toward an anchor or hung to an anchor. A ship, a dove, a light-house tower were also used. The sculptor, however, meant something with more suggestion of art, a genuine work of art, not a mere device; but he had no model.

But one day in church a passage from Luke was read: "And when he hath found it, he layeth it on his shoulders rejoicing." A thought, not from the speaker, flashed into the sculptor's mind. Whether he heard the rest of the sermon, I do not know; but he too went home rejoicing, and began at once to turn over his old patterns till he found what he wanted. He pulled the sheet out; it was of course not Christ; but Hermes (Mercury) the Ram-Bearer, a heathen god carrying a sheep on his shoulder. And how good the tools felt! He was quit of flags and pomegranates for a while. He worked hard, and found himself perhaps a little out of practice, but gradually the figure began to emerge from the block—the drapery and the rough outline first; then the limbs, the sheep, the head. The face was going to be the difficulty; it could not be exactly like Hermes the Ram-Bearer; he must alter it somehow, but he kept it young and beardless. A Christian friend dropped in, and asked in dismay: "Idols again? are you going back?" "No!" said the sculptor; "I'm not going back. You wait and see."

[1] Tertullian, "de Baptismo," 1.

STATUE OF THE GOOD SHEPHERD 197

At last it was done. The Good Shepherd bore a strong likeness to Hermes with the Ram; it was not a very great work of art—it was stiff and conventional, not much better and not much worse than the gods he made of old; but it told a tale. It was not Hermes; it was Christ; and in his rough statue he had embodied three things. The Good Shepherd stood there with the sheep found and on his shoulders; and as the sculptor looked at his poor, homely masterpiece, he could almost fancy the joy in the presence of the angels, he enjoyed it so much himself. He had worked into his statue the gist of the Christian gospel; he could not preach it, perhaps he could not talk about it very clearly or convincingly, but stone and chisel were his medium of expression, and he had made it clear in stone that God had sent the Good Shepherd, and that he is always seeking the lost and finding it. There is an eternal element in an artist's conception, and if his hand and brain did not go paired, his heart had seized the eternal significance of Christ, and his hand had done it into stone; somebody else, with more skill, could improve on it. In the third place—here he had to meet critics who knew the scripture better than he did, and who told him he had confused the Good Shepherd in St. John with the everyday ordinary shepherd in St. Luke; the Good Shepherd in St. John never carried a sheep. "Didn't he?" said the sculptor; "perhaps I have mixed them, then; but my idea of the Good Shepherd was the one who went after the lost sheep till he found it;" and then he added with a sudden flash of modesty and truth: "I wanted to tell my own story too; when I carved the sheep on his shoulders, I thought of all he had done for me."

And here our scrap-work story ends; and we may ask again how much of it is true. It has at any rate so much truth in it, that it was in this way, one by one, the early Christians were won for Jesus Christ, by faithful, dim, obscure people, whose names did not survive, and sometimes (as I think in Tertullian's own case) by the death of the martyrs. The statue of the Good Shepherd is historical, though I do not know exactly the date [1] or place of its making, and no one knows the name of the maker. But consider what he had done. If he had mixed the parables of Jesus, if he had made Christ look surprisingly like a Greek God—one of the devil's angels, if he had had a most pagan zest in handling the old tools till he wondered if his motives were as pure as he hoped—he gave to Art a great type for all that, for he had worked from his heart and wrought a Christian's experience of his Saviour into stone; and every such translation of it is a new Gospel.

[1] There is a statue of the Good Shepherd in the Vatican, which is assigned to the early second century—an earlier date than I have ventured upon. A Terra-cotta of the Shepherd, of the end of the third century, was found in a Christian cemetery at Akhmim (Panopolis).

If he had, as we have imagined, renounced what he loved best in the world for Christ's sake, he had found it again—the lost curves, the lost art, the lost joy of creative work. In any case he gave the Christian Church a new medium, a new voice, and a new and eternal expression of the central truth of the Gospel. The type he made has never died and never will. The man had caught the very thought of Jesus, and embodied it. The Good Shepherd will always for Christian people have the sheep upon his shoulders.

XI

THE RELIGION OF MARTIN LUTHER [1]

I

The term Saint to-day has some implication of anæmia and irrelevance. The word suggests men and women who lived in an old world—or, if they live still, have a sort of half-life in out-of-the-way corners of this world, screened from the knowledge of its mind and its ways; they may have known something of human sin and misery, they may have lived beautiful lives amid squalid surroundings, but all the time they were elsewhere in heart—mystics who dreamed themselves away from our world into some vague Divine love—people for whom the intellect was never a source of trouble—happy strangers in a world of doubt and change, of economic and psychological perplexities—at peace because they escaped all problems. People of another habit, who lived in the thick of the world's battles, who doubted half the time and believed furiously the rest, who fought for their visions and ideals, received blows,

[1] Perhaps I may properly recall that the second part of this paper was an article in *The Student Movement*, written on the suggestion of Dr Alexander Whyte.

and dealt as good or better in return—men of that type, of course, were not saints. St. Paul luckily is so far away in time, and his words so screened by the nimbus of inspiration, that we allow the label to him; he remains a saint because he has ceased to be a man. But if he had lived at the Reformation! "Grand, rough old Martin Luther," as Browning called him (with a hint of patronage in his combination of adjectives), Luther, "whose words were half-battles," as Jean Paul Friedrich Richter said, and who had too Homeric a joy in battle altogether [1]—he does not correspond to our conception of a saint.

Indeed, I have heard it suggested that it is better, generally, *not* to read the *Lives* of men whom we have been taught in childhood to reverence; and it was a *Life of Luther* that prompted the remark. The writer perhaps had aimed too successfully at being colourless; but the critic alleged that it was Luther's own letters that gave him away. To so low an ebb in historical criticism and intelligence have we come, that cultured people seem unable to understand anything but pretty manners and nice thoughts in religion. Many things have contributed to this. We live in an age of uncertainty, when anybody who is definite makes us uncomfortable; just as a child who is trying to be emphatic is told he is rude.

[1] "Dear husband, you are too rude!" said Katie, when he denounced Schwenckfeld as a fool and a maniac in 1543. P. Smith, "Life of Luther," p. 407.

Any emphasis is rude. The idea of Christian charity has been perverted, in reaction against intolerance, to mean a Protagorean acceptance of the equal value of all opinions; but when St. Paul said that Charity believeth all things, he hardly meant this.[1] A Catholic revival, too, has affected English journalists, who are apt to be our spiritual guides—quick, easy, impressionists, with a sympathetic eye for the picturesque and the unusual—and Luther is not very acceptable to them. Many of us have a defective idea of freedom of thought, and use the name for what is simply absence of thought, loose and inconclusive thinking that grapples with nothing and leads nowhere. There is a lack of intellectual discipline in our training—of the realization that truth is not obvious or easy, that conviction is essential to real action and to manhood itself, and that it is only to be reached by a kind of dour, dogged, grim energy of mind. How people of such slack intellectual habits could expect to understand history, it is not easy to explain; it would be more frank to say they have no knowledge of it at all. Religion, again, is no field for the easy-going. Bishop Gore has remarked that men take the love of God as an obvious axiom in religious thought, while it is anything but

---

[1] So much was pointed out by Luther himself. "'You Wittenbergers have no charity!' When we ask what charity is, they say, 'That we should be harmonious in doctrine and abandon those quarrels over religion.'" Luther was quite explicit that charity does not include compromising the claims of Christ or of truth.—M'Giffert, "Life of Luther," p. 326.

obvious or axiomatic; it is a problem, or, if it is a conclusion, it takes a great deal of reaching, as hard to win as the kingdom of God, which, as Jesus said, may need some violence if a man is really to enter it.

Luther is a historical figure, and a man who opened for us new paths in the experience of Jesus Christ. Lord Acton once wrote to Bishop Creighton, and Creighton repeated the question in a letter to Thomas Hodgkin: "What was it that made Luther so great?" They were all three great historians; Hodgkin's answer is not recorded, but both the other two held that it had never been explained. How many people have never asked the question at all! But once a man begins to ask it, and to feel his way to the answer and to divine why Luther was great, he has a prospect at once of a more intelligible view of History, and of a deeper conception of Christianity. For some part of Luther's greatness surely lies in his effectual grasp of the significance of Christ, in his new view of Christ's incredible love and power. When we begin to have glimpses of a Christ on the scale of Luther's Christ, the world, as Paul said, is a new thing, a new creation—amazingly, startlingly new and wonderful.

Other types of religious life have of late been brought before us with singular skill and charm. Few books can, in these respects, rival M. Paul Sabatier's "St. Francis," for instance, and a number of brilliant and able writers have been interpreting Mysticism to us. Few to-day would echo, unqualified or at all, the trenchant words of John Wesley about Jacob Boehme, or Behmen, as he was then called in England: "I object, not only that he is obscure (although even this is an inexcusable fault in a writer on practical religion); not only that his whole hypothesis is unproved; wholly unsupported either by Scripture or reason; but that the ingenious madman over and over contradicts Christian experience, reason, scripture and himself."[1] It does not help Luther with us to be told of his rough speech, of the anger and fury, with which he hewed Casper Schwenckfeld, the mystic, in pieces before the Lord; for, bluntly, we do not quickly see what the quarrel was about; nor, perhaps, did Schwenckfeld. But Luther accused Schwenckfeld of having two Christs[2]; and in the long run the charge does lie against the mystics that their teaching turns attention away from the historical Christ to an experience, which, though they elect to associate it with a peculiar realization of God's love, is susceptible of a quite different interpretation. The mystics are indeed the most dogmatic, and perhaps the least scientific, of men; but the time has not come to be dogmatic on the bases and the explanation of Mysticism. A seventeenth century writer, of little distinction indeed, but an ex-Quaker, laid his finger on an

[1] John Wesley's "Journal," 15th July, 1773 (vol. iii. p. 512; Everyman Edition).
[2] See below, p. 215.

essential weakness.[1] "It was not the light within that was hanged on a tree," he said, but "we came to forget and not regard, nor have faith in, the Crucified Jesus."

"Mysticism," says Rufus Jones, Quaker and scholar, "as a type of religion, has staked its precious realities too exclusively upon the functions of what to-day we call the subconscious. Impressed with the Divine significance of 'inward bubblings,' the mystic has made too slight an account of the testimony of Reason and the contribution of history."[2] That was very much what Luther meant, but belonging to the sixteenth century, and having a genius for incisive speech (and an incurable illness, too, it should be remembered), his language lacked something of our modern scientific poise, and of the repose that marks our caste.

It is good to be often reminded of St. Francis, who loved men—which we may or may not understand—but who also loved Jesus in a way not so instinctive with us. Yet Francis belongs to the middle ages—a period more remote from us than the Athens of Pericles or the Roman Empire of Augustus; and we belong to an age the legitimate heir of the troublesome times of Renaissance and Reformation. It is good to turn again to that *Theologia Germanica,*

[1] Francis Bugg, "The Picture of Quakerism" (1697), p. 23.
[2] Rufus Jones, "Spiritual Reformers in the Sixteenth and Seventeenth Centuries," p. xxviii; a valuable and illuminating book.

which Luther loved and ranked next to the Bible and St. Augustine. But it is good, also, to turn aside and drop in to chat with Luther at his table, to hear him preach, to watch him write—to ride with John Wesley and hear what he has to say to Kingswood colliers—and with them to be brought back to the old words and the old faith: *Et in unum Dominum JESUM CHRISTUM . . . qui propter nos homines et salutem nostram descendit de cœlis et incarnatus est . . . et crucifixus est pro nobis.*[1]

II

In what follows I propose, not, indeed, to answer Acton's question, but to speak of Luther's religion, as it finds expression in his table talk and in passages of his writings that have stayed with me, and which I have been glad to remember; to try to give some picture of what he felt and believed, of what was the real stimulus to his controversies, but, much more, was the life-nerve of all he did and was. To set him among the men of his day, their methods, thoughts, doubts and discoveries, their wars and politics, and to see how he handles the life of man on the basis of his own experience of what Jesus Christ could be for a man—these are larger tasks, fit work for the specialist, who is at once historian

[1] Hahn, "Bibliothek der Symbole," No. 76.

THE RELIGION OF MARTIN LUTHER 207

and theologian, and loves Christ as Luther did. Our present endeavour should be more compassable.[1]

The song in *Faust* suggests that Luther was fat and gross—a fate which sometimes overtakes us in later life, and it appears that Luther grew stout in old age. But Lucas Cranach, who painted him several times in middle life, drew a lean man of ascetic appearance. He is thus described about 1522: "With deep brown-black eyes, flashing and sparkling like a star, so that you could not easily bear their gaze . . . by nature a friendly and accessible man . . . his earnestness was so mingled with joy and kindliness that it was a pleasure to live with him."[2] Nearly everyone who has described him was impressed by the restless fire that flashed from his eyes.[3] He scandalized Europe by marrying a nun, but he recaptured family life for religion by doing it.

A great, strong, hearty, nonsensical,[4] shrewd,

[1] In what follows, references to M'Giffert and Preserved Smith are to their "Lives of Luther"; Lindsay, "Reformation," explains itself; "Erlangen" means the great German edition of Luther's works; "Table Talk" is Luther's Table Talk (Tischreden), translated by Henry Bell, three centuries ago (Henry Bell, translated from the German edition of 1574, Frankfurt; his actual copy is in the Library of Sidney Sussex College, Cambridge); "Galatians," the Commentary on that Epistle; Herrmann is Herrmann's "Communion of the Christian with God," to which I owe many quotations (and a very great deal else); Currie, "Selection of Luther's Letters" (in English); Förstemann, edition of Luther's "Tischreden" (1844).

[2] M'Giffert, p. 240.
[3] P. Smith, p. 316.
[4] His fun, P. S. Smith, 345.

charming, truculent character, he survives in the reminiscences of his friends and in his own letters. A well-known couplet preserves what he thought of the man who loves not woman, wine and song; and in more serious mood he said, "Next to theology, it is to music I give the highest place and the greatest honour."[1] He loved books, and poetry, and German ballads,[2] and Cicero,[3] and chess,[4] and birds, and animals, and children, and common people, and beggars, and all sorts of things. He wrote jolly letters to his wife, "my Lord Katie," with religion and nonsense, and piety and fun mixed—letters exactly like himself, boyish to the last. Some of the most nonsensical and boyish of his letters were written to cheer her up, while he was away on that last journey, in the course of which he died; "To the saintly anxious lady," he began, "most saintly doctoress."[5] He rallied his friends and joked about himself—what a talker he *had been*, and so on; he even talked nonsense about martyrdom, when his friends told him he was heading straight for it—"nettles wouldn't be so bad, one could stand them; but to be burned with fire,—no, that would be too hot."[6] Incidentally, as

[1] d'Aubigné, iii. 241. *Cf.* P. Smith, 346.
[2] Ballads, P. Smith, 344, 345; letter to Wenzel Link, 2 Mch. 1535.
[3] Of Cicero, "I hope God will be merciful to him." "Table Talk," p. 509. P. Smith, 342.
[4] M'Giffert, 299.
[5] Currie, No. 499.
[6] M'Giffert, p. 197.

we all know, he made new eras in religion and history and criticism. Altogether he is what I have heard called "a great human"—one of the very greatest, and it all centres in his religion.

Luther was one of those real men who build on experience and not on theory. He flung himself as a monk into religious devotion, and did lasting injury to his health by his austerities. "The truth is," he said afterwards, "I was a pious monk, and I held my rule so strongly that I can say, 'If a monk ever reached heaven by monkery, I would have found my way there also'; all my convent comrades will bear witness to that."[1] But his conscience never found peace in it all, nor elsewhere, till he realized the great fact which he summed up in the doctrine of Justification by Faith—the fact that it is God Who gives and not man who works out Salvation—that Salvation is just taking with a loving heart what God in His great love wants to give to you, and simply living in the assurance, conscious or subconscious all the time, that God in Christ has proved His love of you. That is the hard thing to believe, for, as he said, "We are always wanting to turn the tables and do good to that poor man, our Lord God, from whom we are rather to receive it."[2] It is the other way round—"before thou callest upon God or seekest Him, God must have come to thee and found thee."

[1] Lindsay, "Reformation," i. 427; Erlangen, 31, 273.
[2] Herrmann, p. 213; Erlangen, 49, 343.

And it is not mere intellectual assent to doctrines, but letting oneself go on God [1]—"There are many of you who say, 'Christ is a man of this kind: He is God's Son, was born of a pure virgin, became man, died, rose again from the dead,' and so forth; *that is all nothing*. But when we truly say that He is Christ, we mean that He was given for us without any works of ours, that without any merits of ours He has won for us the Spirit of God, and has made us children of God; so that we might have a gracious God, might with Him be lords over all things in heaven and on earth, and, besides, might have eternal life through Christ—that is faith, and that is true knowledge of Christ." [2] When he was a monk, he says,[3] "When I prayed, or when I said mass, I used to add this in the end: 'O Lord Jesus, I come unto Thee, and I pray Thee that these burdens and this straightness of my rule and religion may be a full recompense for all my sins.'" But, as he says elsewhere,[4] "a believing soul ought to talk with our Saviour Christ in this manner: 'Lord! I am *thy sins*, Thou art *my Righteousness;* therefore am I

---

[1] Die aber Gott glauben die wagens auf Gott, und setzen alles dahin in Gottes Gewalt, dass er es mache nach seinem Gefallen. Erlangen, vol. 13, p. 252. Aber sich bloss an Christum hängen, durch den Glauben, als in dem wir, ohn alle unser Werk und Verdienst, Gottes Gnad und ewiges Leben haben, das ist nicht Menschen-sondern Gottes-Werk. Erlangen, 50, 241.

[2] Herrmann, p. 161.

[3] "Galatians," fol. 76 *a*.

[4] "Table Talk," p. 138; Förstemann, vol. i. p. 385, No. 115.

joyful, and boldly do triumph; for my sins do not over-balance Thy Righteousness, neither will Thy Righteousness suffer me to be or remain a sinner. Blessed and praised be Thy holy Name (sweet Jesus) for evermore.'" Righteousness does not come from good works, but *vice versa;* "the tree maketh the apple, but not the apple the tree." [1]

Everything turns on the Incarnation, but the Incarnation does not begin with a doctrine and an abstract noun—it begins with a baby. "Begin thou there where Christ began," says Luther,[2] in other words inculcating what we have to learn, viz., that fact precedes theory, even if it be dogma, and that History comes before Theology—the history of Christ, the history of the Church, and the history of you and me. Thus, said Luther,[3] "Without Christ we cannot know God. . . . The Father Himself is too high; therefore He saith, 'I will show you a way whereby you may come unto Me, namely, Christ; believe in Him, depend on Him, and then in due time ye shall well find who I am.'" Luther would not have men in any case dispute of predestination, and he used to quote a saying of Staupitz, "If thou wilt needs dispute concerning the same, then, I truly advise thee, to begin first at the wounds of Christ, as then all that disputation will cease and have an

---

[1] "Galatians," fol. 84 *a.*
[2] "Galatians," fol. 16 *b.*
[3] "Table Talk," p. 140; Förstemann, vol. i. p. 390, No. 120.

end therewith."[1] "True Christian Divinity (as I give you often warning) setteth not God unto us in His majesty ... It commandeth us not to search out the nature of God, but to know His will set out to us in Christ." "Wherefore whensoever thou art occupied in the matter of thy salvation, setting aside all curious speculation of God's unsearchable majesty, all cogitations of works, of traditions, of philosophy, yea, and of God's law too, run straight to the manger and embrace this Infant, and the Virgin's little babe in thine arms, and behold Him as He was born, sucking, growing up, conversant among men, teaching, dying, rising again, ascending up above all the heavens, and having power above all things. By this means shalt thou be able to shake off all terrors and errors, like as the sun driveth away the clouds. And this sight and contemplation will keep thee in the right way that thou mayest follow whither Christ is gone."[2] Some of my readers may recall Spenser's *Hymne of Heavenly Love*:

Beginne from first, where he encradled was
In simple cratch, wrapt in a wad of hay,
Betweene the toylefull Oxe and humble Asse,
And in what rags, and in how base aray,
The glory of our heauenly riches lay,
When him the silly Shepheards came to see,
Whom greatest Princes sought on lowest knee.

From thence reade on the storie of his life,
His humble carriage, his vnfaulty wayes,

[1] "Table Talk," p. 405; Förstemann, iii. p. 160, No. 75.
[2] "Galatians," fol. 17 b.

His cancred foes, his fights, his toyle, his strife,
His paines, his pouertie, his sharpe assayes,
Through which he past his miserable dayes,
Offending none, and doing good to all,
Yet being malist both of great and small.

And looke at last how of most wretched wights,
He taken was, betrayd, and false accused,
How with most scornefull taunts, and fell despights
He was reuyld, disgrast, and foule abused,
How scourgd, how crownd, how buffeted, how brused
And lastly how twixt robbers crucifyde,
With bitter wounds through hands, through feet and syde.

I have sometimes wondered whether Spenser had seen the passage of Luther, for I have transcribed it from a copy of the second edition of the English translation of the *Commentary on Galatians*, first published in 1575; and Spenser was of the Puritan party. "Try," writes Luther to Melanchthon (13 Jan. 1522), "not to hear of Jesus in glory till thou have seen Him crucified." All this is no mere record of the past—"to me it is not simply an old song of an event that happened 1500 years ago . . . it is a gift and a bestowing that endures for ever."[1]

The essence of the whole matter is that Christ belongs to and cares for the individual man. "Christ, when He cometh, is nothing else but joy and sweetness to a trembling and broken heart, as here Paul witnesseth, who setteth Him out in this most sweet and comfortable title, when he saith: 'Which loved me and gave Himself for me.' Christ

[1] Herrmann, p. 186.

therefore is in very deed a lover of those which are in trouble and anguish, and sin and death, and such a lover as gave Himself for us. . . . Read therefore with great vehemency these words *me* and *for me*."[1] It had been with him a temptation to think that God hated sinners and himself among them; so when such thoughts daunt him, he turns, and bids us turn, to Christ:—"Dost thou see nothing but the law, sin, terror, heaviness, temptation, death, hell and the devil? . . . Trouble me no more, O my soul . . . say 'Lady Law, thou art not alone, neither art thou all things, but besides three there are yet other things much greater and better than thou art, namely, grace, faith and blessing,' and all because of Christ."[2] As he dwells on the thought of the Incarnation, he feels anew the wonder of it, the impossibility, as we do— "the greatest work of wonder which ever was done on earth is that the only begotten Son of God died the most contemned death upon the Cross. It is to us a wonder above all wonders that the Father should say to His only Son (who by nature is God), 'Go Thy way, let them hang Thee on the Gallows.' "[3]

It is this realization of a personal relation with God in Christ, in a crucified and risen Christ, that is the nerve of his controversies. The Pope, it was believed, could by a stroke of the pen, prevent a

---

[1] "Galatians," fol. 88 *b*.
[2] "Galatians," fol. 170 *a*.
[3] "Table Talk," p. 134. Förstemann, vol. i. p. 376, No. 106.

whole nation from approaching God; an *interdict* meant spiritual death.[1] How could it be so, when one "read with great vehemency that *me* and *for me?*" Luther stood for the priesthood of all believers—"a Christian man is the most free lord of all and subject to none," he wrote, and his next sentence developed his meaning: "A Christian man is the most dutiful servant of all, and subject to every one." (That is the apple, and the former is the tree.) That is no doubt why he says, "When I am in the pulpit, then I resolve to preach only to men and maidservants; I would not make a step into the pulpit for the sakes of Philip Melanchthon, Justus Jonas, or the whole University." [2] "Thoughts are tax-free," he quoted, but when Schwenckfeld, the mystic, expounded his thoughts, Luther would have none of them—"he makes two Christs . . . one who hangs on the Cross and the other who has ascended into Heaven and sits at the right hand of the Heavenly Father; he says I must not pray to the Christ who hangs on the Cross and walks on earth." [3] There he is—back to the actual and historical, his feet on the fact! And to others who spoke of revelations and visions and voices and the like, he could say, "If it were in my hand, I would not wish God

[1] T. M. Lindsay, "Reformation," vol. i. p. 440.
[2] "Table Talk," p. 289. Förstemann, ii. p. 412, No. 97. M'Giffert, p. 319.
[3] P. Smith, pp. 406-7.

to speak to me from heaven or to appear to me."[1]
"I have (God be praised) learned so much of Him
[Christ] out of the Scriptures, that I am well and
thoroughly satisfied; therefore I desire neither to
see nor to hear Him corporally."[2] Monks and
prophets may claim these visions; for him the speech
of God in facts suffices—and how much it is, when
one realizes it as he did! It is interesting at the
same time to find that he has reached the modern
point of view about psychological "experiences,"
viz., that they really add very little to anybody, and
cannot be relied on as new sources of truth.

No, the Christ who gave Himself for me ("read
it with great vehemency") is also the risen Christ,
and that means a life of freedom and happiness for
those He loves. "Christ comes and sits at the right
hand, *not* of the Kaiser (*Cæsaris*)—in that case we
should have perished long since—but at the right
hand of God. This is an incredible great thing.
Still, I delight in it, incredible as it is, and I mean
to die in it. Then why should I not also live in it?
... If He has lost His title (King of kings) in
Augsburg, He must also have lost it in heaven and
on earth." So he wrote to Justus Jonas.[3] At table
he put it in a grotesque way [4]—"When Christ speak-

[1] Herrmann, p. 188.
[2] "Table Talk," p. 138.
[3] To Jonas, 9 July 1530; Currie, No. 231, where a good deal of it is mistranslated, however.
[4] "Table Talk," p. 143. Förstemann (1844), vol. i. p. 397, § 132.

eth a word, He openeth a mouth which is as big as heaven and earth. . . . When the emperor speaketh a word it is held of some value; but when Christ speaketh, He taketh up at one bit heaven and earth. Therefore must we regard this man's words otherwise than the words of emperors, popes, etc., for He is true, and very God." "Does *He* talk to the wind?" he asks Melanchthon (27 June 1530) in one of a number of letters full of faith and courage and gaiety; "What fear is there for truth if He reigns? . . . It is your philosophy that troubles you so, not your Theology. . . . He who has become our Father will be the Father of our children. . . . As for our cause, for my part (whether it is dulness or the Spirit, let Christ see to it), I am not much disturbed; nay! I have better hope than I had hoped to have."[1] "If Moses had waited to understand to the very end how he was to escape Pharaoh's army, Israel would perhaps be in Egypt to this day."[2] "Lately, I saw two wonders. The first, when I looked out of the window and saw the stars in heaven, and the whole beautiful dome of God, and yet I saw no pillars on which the Master had set his dome; and still the heaven did not fall and the dome stands firm. Now there are some people who are looking for such pillars, and would like to touch them and feel them; and because they cannot, they

---

[1] Currie, No. 225.
[2] To Melanchthon, 29 June 1530; Currie, No. 226.

fidget and tremble, as if the heaven would certainly fall, for no other reason than that they neither feel nor see the pillars. If they could feel the pillars, the heaven would be safe enough!"[1]

With a faith like this in Christ at God's right hand, he can face everything—Duke Georges by the reservoirful[2]—a devil on every tile in Worms, martyrdom, anything,—yes, and temptations and troubles of every sort. "The best way to drive out the fiend is to despise him and call on Christ, for he cannot bear that. You should say to him, 'If *you* are lord over Christ, so be it!' That is what I said at Eisenach"[3]—which is an even better way of dealing with him than throwing an inkpot at him. "In temptation we must in no wise judge thereof according to our own sense and feeling. . . . Wherefore in the midst of thy temptation and infirmity cleave only unto Christ and groan unto Him; He giveth the Holy Ghost which crieth *Abba Father*. . . . The Spirit maketh intercession for us in our temptation, not with many words or long prayer . . . but only uttereth a little sound and a feeble groaning, as *Ah Father!* This is but a little word, and yet notwithstanding it comprehended all things. The mouth speaketh not, but the affection of the heart speaketh after this manner: 'Although I be oppressed with anguish and terror on every side, and seem to be

[1] To Brück, 5 Aug. 1530; Currie, No. 238.
[2] Letter of 5 March 1522, and Carlyle's Essay on "Heroes."
[3] P. Smith, p. 126.

forsaken and utterly cast away from Thy presence, yet am I Thy child, and Thou art my Father for Christ sake; I am beloved because of the Beloved.' "[1]

"Whatever comes or shall come or happen, by prayer, which is alone the all-powerful Empress in human affairs, we shall manage everything, by her we shall steer our plans, correct mistakes, put up with what we cannot mend, conquer all that is evil, keep all that is good—as we have done already down to this present, and learnt the power of prayer."[2] In this way and in this spirit all duty may be faced, little and big. If it comes to martyrdom, "my head is a little thing compared with Christ, who was slain with the utmost ignominy. . . . This is no place for weighing risk and safety; no, we must take care, on the contrary, not to abandon to the contempt of the wicked the Gospel, once we have taken it up, nor to give the adversaries cause to glory over us, because we do not dare to confess what we have taught, and fear to shed our blood for it—such cowardice on our part, such triumph on theirs, Christ in His mercy avert. Amen."[3] If it is the daily round and common task, "what you do in your house is worth as much as if you did it up in Heaven for our Lord God. . . . It looks like a small thing when a maid cooks and cleans and does other housework. But because God's command is there, even such a lowly

[1] "Galatians," fol. 191 *b*, 192 *a*.
[2] Letter to Melanchthon, 8 April 1540; Currie, No. 403.
[3] Letter to Spalatin, 21 Dec. 1520; Currie, No. 51.

employment must be praised as a service of God, far surpassing the holiness and asceticism of all monks and nuns. Here there is no command of God. But there God's command is fulfilled, that one should honour Father and Mother and help in the care of the house." [1] "It is not humility," he said, "if you know you are humble."

There is a religion—Christ at God's right hand still, Who loved me and gave Himself for me, and a duster or a pen in my hand, and a bit of work to do for Him. "He loadeth no heavy burdens upon us ... but will only have that we believe in Him and preach of Him [glauben und reden]. But thou mayst be sure and certain that thou shall be plagued and persecuted therefore; and therefore our sweet and blessed Saviour [der treue liebe Herr], giveth unto us a comfortable promise, where He saith, 'I will be with you in the time of trouble and will help you out,' etc. (Luke xii. 17). I (said Luther) make no such promise to my servant when I set him to work, either to plow or to cart; but Christ will help me in my need." [2]

[1] M'Giffert, p. 177, from a sermon.
[2] "Table Talk," p. 132. Förstemann, i. p. 372, No. 100.

XII

A LOST ARTICLE OF FAITH

I

The old Scottish Christianity owed not a little of its rugged strength to its firm and clear apprehension of the reality of God's judgment. The vivid picture drawn in the Apocalypse haunted the imagination and the memory. There stood the Great White Throne, and on it sat One, from whose face the earth and the heaven fled away, and there was found no place for them; but man, in all his guilt and triviality, had to confront that face and look it straight between the eyes. An awful prospect it was for the best of men, but it gave intensity and depth to life. All things had to be viewed *sub specie æternitatis*—how would they look in eternity? against *that* background? before *that* throne? However they might look thus set at last, a man of sense would wish to see them so here and now. And the deeper men always tended to see them so.

Hence came much of the Scottish character. Accustomed to look things through and through, the Scot had a way of getting to the bottom of whatever he had in mind. Even before John Knox and the Reformation Scotland had treated Philosophy more seriously than England ever has, with an emphasis on the moral side of it, which Latin Christianity has always had from Augustine and Tertullian onward. Life, character, society, nation, must rest on the ultimate. If the satirist find the real national anthem of England in the well-known doggerel—

> God bless the squire and his rich relations,
> And teach us poor our proper stations—

to a man who was conscious that the squire, or laird, and he himself must stand on one footing before that face, from whose aspect heaven and earth and landed possessions would have fled away, and be gone forever, the distinctions of earth would wear very thin. And, for good or ill, they did wear thin, and there has never been in Scotland that deference to position which was long familiar in England. And what was true of the squire, was true of priest and minister. Men were driven into independence of mind as well as into self-criticism; and the consciousness that the distinction between right and wrong, between truth and error, is fundamental and eternal gave stamina to both habits.

It was not peculiar to Scotland, this clear vision of the Judgment Day. Tertullian knew it and drew it in a terrible picture. The early Christian had it, owing something to Jewish and something to Greek

A LOST ARTICLE OF FAITH

thinkers. The misery of life, the uncertainty of it, the flaunting triumph of violence in the age after Alexander had driven the Jews of the period to postulate another life, where the contrast between right and wrong would be brought into clear relief for ever, by a judgment of God that should at once rid man of his doubts and God of all hint of indifference. Thought was impossible on other lines. Plato, says Mr. R. W. Livingstone,[1] was "a Christian born out of due time. His race had held that human nature was fundamentally good, and thought that knowledge and training would abolish wrong. Plato argued that there is an incurably evil element in man to which only death can put an end; as the Church argued that there is an incurably evil element in him, which can only be quenched by the grace of God. Plato's race had held that physical beauty is among the highest objects of desire. Plato himself thought that the body interferes with the soul, often encrusts and embrutes it. He taught men to shun its vanities and affections, to leave even politics and public life, to devote themselves to the contemplation of God and the saving of their souls. Plato told his disciples to look forward to a future life, to a judgment to come, to heaven, hell or purgatory, to a scheme of punishments and rewards that followed

---

[1] "The Greek Genius and its Meaning for Us," p. 195. I have taken the freedom of leaving out some sentences or half sentences, but without changing the meaning of the passage.

a man's conduct in his time on earth. Plato's race had a generous confidence in human nature. Original sin, asceticism, ideas of a future life, strict authoritarianism—in all these Plato anticipated the mediæval Church."

So Mr. Livingstone sums up Plato, and then adds comment, which I take leave to quote. "Whether he is right in his view of human nature, is one of the great unsolved questions of the world, and not the least interest of his writings is that they raise it so clearly. . . . Our own age [1912] would probably decide against him. Things are well with it. It is making money fast; education and recreation are cheap; science has removed many causes of misery; savagery and revolution are rare; so at present we are riding high on a wave of humanism, and are optimistic about the nature of man, and the rapidity of the march on Paradise." In a book published since the European War Professor J. B. Bury has subjected these ideas of ours to historical inquiry;[1] whence came our belief in inevitable progress? how old is it? And it appears that it is scarcely two centuries old and depends a good deal on loose thinking about the progress in scientific discovery and the application of natural laws to economic processes. Altogether the evidence for rejecting Plato's view of human nature is not complete, and Plato

[1] "The Idea of Progress."

would still urge that the distinction between right and wrong, between truth and error, is more inevitable than human progress, and is independent of it.

II

The century, which has seen the swiftest progress in mechanical contrivance and the adjustment of Nature to comfort, has also seen great changes in Christian thought, not all of which however are to be associated with that progress. There have been growth and development in other ways. A closer study of archæology has shed much light upon Biblical history, and new canons of historical criticism have come in. New knowledge of non-Christian religion and non-European thought have modified men's views. Above all the return to fact has concentrated Christian students upon the life and mind of Jesus Christ. There has been a relative decline in the attention given to Systematic Theology and a great heightening of interest in the personality of Jesus. The old view of the verbal inspiration of the Bible is hardly held to-day among educated people; its going has relieved Christian thinkers of many difficulties which had no existence apart from this dogma. The conception of a progressive knowledge of God was an immense gain. Inspiration had in the past been regarded in a mechanical way; and men feel that the inspired writer is of all men least mechanical and above other men sensitive and individual. These characteristics were found in different measure in different authors and periods of the Bible; and more stress is now laid on those where the new view enables men to feel the greater depth, the truer and higher realization of God; and a new freedom has followed. With the old theory of inspiration there have faded away other tenets, which, as generally presented, rested latterly rather on the presumption that "the Scripture cannot be broken" than on their value to the Christian soul or their congruity with the known character of Jesus of Nazareth. The very statement that "the Scripture cannot be broken" coming from the fourth gospel required re-examination; what was its origin, its meaning? What exactly was Scripture? Which books for instance, Ecclesiastes or Ecclesiasticus? and what was to be understood by its breaking? The new standard was pre-eminently that of consistency with the nature and teaching of Jesus.

The children's hymn, resting on abundant Gospel warrant and historically sound, had emphasized the "gentle Jesus"; it was, as far as it went, a true picture. The dogma of an irrevocable hell that awaited the unconverted, whatever his opportunities or his lack of them, immediately on death, had less warrant in the teaching of Jesus. Both conceptions must, it was taught, be held; but it was done by that human habit of thinking in compartments, which we feel to

A LOST ARTICLE OF FAITH 227

be illegitimate, and yet to which men have often owed their sense and their sanity. Two ideas may seem to be in conflict, because neither is quite grasped, and because their relation is not firmly understood.

With the change in the view of inspiration, the closer knowledge of other religions, and the deepening realization of the character of Jesus issuing in new love for him and a new acceptance of him, the terrible doctrine of endless hell, which after all had really implied the defeat of every purpose Jesus had set before him and the invalidity of his most fundamental beliefs, faded out of men's minds. It was a real gain; but spiritual gains, like other gains, are achieved and held with danger. Freedom is one thing for the man who understands its cost, its opportunities and responsibilities, and another for him who does not. Before negro emancipation in America, Lowell's "pious editor" maintained that

> Liberty's a kind of thing
> That don't agree with niggers;

and what was Lowell's sarcasm is the political reflection of many Southerners and others after the event. Freedom is a good thing, the greatest of blessings, but it has had ill consequences for those who were not trained to think deeply about it, and to use it aright. The variant in St. Luke in the Bezan Codex attributes this very idea to Jesus:

"Man, if thou knowest what thou dost, blessed art thou, but if thou knowest not, thou art accursed and a transgressor of the law." Misuse of freedom by the negro was the nemesis of his enslavement.

The gain in the newer thought of God was very great indeed for those who took Jesus seriously; for others its consequences were less happy; and in many minds there are both strains—seriousness co-existing with the natural desire to take things easily. For now came the nemesis of thinking in compartments and of holding ideas imperfectly realized. The picture of the "gentle Jesus" remained on one side of their minds for some people, and on the other side nothing or very little. The adjective swamped the substantive; the historical Jesus was lost in the sentimentalist's half picture. The real features of Jesus' mind were not studied; and a vague notion of "Christian charity," a still vaguer one of "forgiveness," prevailed; and the moral stamina was so far gone from popular Christianity.

He's a good fellow, and 'twill all be well!

says one of the pots about the potter in Omar Khayyam's "Rubaiyyat"; and it sums up only too adequately the common theology, sheer travesty as it is of everything we find in the thought of Jesus.

This growing belief, helped by the modern faith in the inevitable march of human progress, cut across all sound thinking and across action. In the older days, for instance, the call to the mission field, to the propagation of the faith, rang like the tocsin in revolutionary Paris for insistence and meaning. Moment by moment, it was urged, souls were passing to the unthinkable for want of what Christians could bring them. This was not precisely the teaching of Jesus; but it put in a terrible way, an exaggerated way if you like, a truth that is real enough —the moral and spiritual bankruptcy of heathen and animistic religious ideas. To-day no one uses the old call; and many readers will at once reject even the qualified account I have given of the fact behind it. The heathen are not counted to be in any very special peril; it is surmised that they have developed their own religions in conformity with their own spiritual experience, habits of thought and needs; no religion or philosophy, it is urged, has ever held men over long tracts of time and wide areas of the world without elements of truth; and it would follow that by some slow process of evolution heathendom is slowly but surely making its way to the same heavenly Father as Christendom:

He's a good fellow, and 'twill all be well!

and perhaps he is every whit as pleased with the animist as with the Christian, with Animism as with Christianity. A new attitude of sympathy to alien cults is not to be deprecated; anything that prompts to intelligence of other men's ideas is doubly helpful

—to the man who understands and to the people understood. But it cannot be said that the "good fellow" theology, as a rule, has either rested on intelligence of the people or matters pronounced upon, or led to it.

The "good fellow" conception of God has also in practice, as it was bound to do, encouraged men and women (I do not know which more) to drop self-criticism and to improvise life as pleasantly as possible in such directions as the moment might suggest.

> Myself will to my darling be
> Both law and impulse.

To what that leads, Plato long ago showed in his appalling picture of the "democratic man" whose soul is a democracy drunk with the strong wine of freedom, where every appetite, every passion, every notion is a citizen as well qualified as any other to take the lead.[1] Plato may be accused of travesty, if he really meant this as a picture of the Athenian citizen of his day; but he is drawing a type which is not unfamiliar to us. The real fault which Plato finds with the man of this character is that he has thought nothing out, that he has no principles, no clear idea of right or wrong, of truth or error, that he associates no permanent value with the distinction between them.

[1] *Cf.* Plato, "Rep.," viii. 557, 558, 562-565.

III

In the modern line of thought, which I have been describing, there are a number of assumptions not verified, nor indeed very closely examined—mere assertions taken to be self-evident, but on examination a good deal less certain. The Hindu always tells you that you can go to Calcutta by rail or river or road; and he appears to hold that that justifies your travelling by the least reliable and the least direct of routes. It is not always certain that you can get to Calcutta by river, for instance, but it is certain that it will take you a long time in any case; and the argument overlooks the desirability of reaching Calcutta quickly, whatever it is, and the advantage, if any, of being there. It is not clear that the heathen is better qualified for working out his own salvation to-day than were the Celts and Saxons of our British Islands in the fifth and sixth centuries. We owe a great deal to those possibly very dogmatic and crude Christian missionaries who believed Christ, even as they conceived of him, to be of more value than the *sidhe* of the Celt and the Odin and Thor of the Saxon. They were right.

There is a good deal in practice to be said for a philosophy that imposes upon you intellectual and other effort as against one that frees you from it. You are more liable to think twice about it. "Evolution" is a word much on our lips, and it has been applied to every aspect of human life as well as to religion. But it is growingly clear that the word is loosely used. Dr. Johnson would get very cross with one of his old lady pensioners, because, whenever he wanted her to be "categorical," she was "wiggle-waggle." Poor old thing! she was afraid of her benefactor, and, like so many of her people, still more afraid of coming to grips with an idea. Even in the physical world, in the region of biology, it would appear that evolution is rather a working hypothesis for a certain section of the field, than a law definitely ascertained and understood in detail. In the region of thought it stands on a similar footing —it is a suggestion, an attractive suggestion, which illustrates a good deal of the known history of thought, provided you give the term the meaning proper to the subject. But in thought, politics, economics, and religion people use the term without proper limitation. The popular mind is more optimistic about evolution than the scientific.[1] Even in biology, I understand, it is not suggested, as amateur biologists might suppose, that the chimpanzees, give them time, will develop into a race that produces Shakespeares and Isaiahs even better than ours; still less—their shape, of course, is against it—will the camels. Whatever was true of their remotest ancestors, these creatures appear to have made their way deep into blind alleys, and I do not gather that

[1] *Cf.* Bury, "Idea of Progress," p. 335.

biologists are very hopeful that their stocks will ever seriously set themselves to retrace their steps. There is the real issue. Whether you use the term evolution or not, it is historically established that all human progress is associated with intellectual choice and intellectul effort, and both of them are apt to be also moral and individual choice and effort.

Apply this to religion, and it ceases to be so clear that "all will yet be well," if you let everything drift, either for other people or for yourself. For, it may be noted, if it is right to let the heathen drift on notions which he inherits or picks up, it cannot be quite right to educate your own children. I am not sure that I am not anticipated here by theorists who hold, against Solomon and Socrates and other authorities, that children do better without guidance or discipline, though this, oddly, is more true of their minds than of their bodies. The body is more obviously than the mind amenable to sepsis. There are backwaters in religion, and blind alleys in thought which lead nowhere, and one great part of human experience has been to ticket them. Some experiments in conduct hardly need to be repeated; there have been enough experiments in theft, murder and adultery; and all over the world men are agreed that there is no "evolution" by those routes. Animism historically does not mean progress as Christianity has meant it; and if God is as pleased with the one as with the other, then one feels there is something wrong with His thinking, a conclusion which one is reluctant to accept. It is another proposition altogether to say that He is as pleased with Animist as with Christian; it is not necessarily true, and it requires examination and definition before we can accept it. It depends a good deal on what the particular Animist and the particular Christian under consideration are doing with their inherited ideas.

IV

It is worthy of remark, and it is perhaps a little curious, that the term "reversion" never became so popular as "evolution." Perhaps the thing seemed less established to the man of science; certainly its explanation was not obvious when the term was first offered to the world. Progress, however, filled the air, and the popular notion of evolution squared with the popular notion of progress.

It is well for men to believe in the possibility of progress and achievement. So much done, so much solid gain made—and men begin to think relapse no longer to be feared. But when we turn to History, it gives us pause; the past, as Mark Twain said, in one of his philosophic moments, which were many and seldom cheerful, the past is "so damned humiliating." The story of Greece and Rome is full of cruelty—civil strife in Greece meant murder, conquest by Rome meant Verres, oppression and slavery. But when Christianity ousts the republican Sulla and the imperial Maximin, we may hope for better things, and we find—Constantius. But he was a heretic; and the Catholic Church triumphant gives us Cortes and Pizarro and their hideous aggression in the name of Christ, and the Bartholomew massacre—and the papal medal of Gregory XIII. commemorating it—and all this after what we call the Renaissance. Monarchy and oppression may be supposed to go hand in hand; a French republic sets up the guillotine and an American republic burns negroes alive by the hundred every year. The Reform Bill was to solve England's problems, and there are still men who complain that our social structure is in ruins. Where greater freedom reigns, Tammany Hall and trusts crush purity and personal liberty. It seems that as soon as we defeat one of the devil's legions, he has another entrenched on a line not very far away.

It is easy to say that, while this is all true about History, it is not the whole truth; the Christian Empire did secure certain things for the lowly that Rome, pagan and noble, never gave—the slave was better treated, the ideal of chastity was higher. *Imperialis verecundia* would have been an epigram in Tacitus; it was historical record in Ammianus Marcellinus. Cortes was an adventurer, and his conquest of Mexico an outrage on the name of Christ; but at least human sacrifice was abolished, even if habitual civil war and the exploitation of the Indian replace it to-day. The French republic has done more for the people than the monarchy did, though it has been less brilliant. The American republic has given new hopes and happier homes to millions of white people, and it did set the negro free at endless cost to itself. That is all right enough; but what is the insidious thing in progress that makes it so necessary for us to apologize for it? Why is the hour of victory so fatal to ideals?

It means that the popular notion of to-day, that progress is simple and inevitable evolution, will not hold; that human nature cannot be counted upon, without the stimulus of an adventure, an enthusiasm, an ideal; that, in one form, if not in another, there is always an element of evil to be reckoned with, to be battled with; and that life is a harder and more difficult campaign than optimists allow—horribly hard, to the verge of despair. A large part of the Christian world has been simply playing with thought; and non-Christians have been alive to the facts which Christians have missed. Virgil knew long ago—living in the country and among farmers, of course he knew how a farm will go back to the wild and plants degenerate:

> Yet can I witness that the plant declines,
> Though long-time chosen, conned with utmost care,
> If human energy and human hands
> Fail to search out the fittest year by year.

A LOST ARTICLE OF FAITH

> So are we doomed to speed from bad to worse,
> Ever borne backwards, drifting whence we came,
> As one whose oars can scarcely hold his boat
> Against the stream, who haply slacks his grip,
> Then headlong down the torrent is he swept
> By the mid-flood.[1]

The keynote of his poem is given later—in a line of rhythm unusual but suggestive:

> *Scilicet omnibus est labor impendendus.*[2]

A gospel of ceaseless work is what he preaches, a long, a lifelong battle with nature in the physical world—with nature who will assuredly undo all you have done if you let it alone. So far are we in the physical world from inevitable progress and safety from reaction. And no one who has treated the training of character seriously can suppose things different there.

No! not easy victory and the comparative insignificance of evil. Plato, the great Hindu teachers, the Stoics, all recognize the seriousness of evil. Instead of a god who is "a good fellow—and 'twill all be well," they find inexorable law in the Universe. "The mills of God grind slowly, but they grind exceeding small" is only a monotheistic rendering of a Greek proverb. While popular Christianity underestimates sin, outsiders, with their eyes on nature's law, say there is no forgiveness of sin any more than

[1] Virgil, "Georgics," i. 197-203; Lord Burghclere's translation, p. 27.
[2] Virgil, "Georgics," ii. 61.

there is a theological or magical remedy for physical infection. A drunkard produces in himself a certain permanent condition; a change of opinion will not alter his physical decrepitude, they urge—though they may be undervaluing conviction as a means to a change of life which will mend him gradually. "Injustice," says Carlyle, "always repays itself with frightful compound interest."

The universe of the modern fatalist is in any case more wholesome and habitable than the impossible and fundamentally immoral affair that some Christians make of God's world, with the amiable nonentity of their imagination in charge of it, who will stand anything and never mind it, whose laws work off and on, and who has so general a benevolence for right and wrong that he does not notice any particular difference between them. A Scottish satirist [1] has hit this figure off exactly; the old beadle is criticizing the new minister and his new God:

> A God wha wadna fricht the craws;
> A God wha never lifts the tawse;
> Wha never heard o' Moses' laws
>   On stane or paper;
> A kind o' thowless Great First Cause
>   Skinklin' through vapour.
>
> The auld blue Hell he thinks a haver;
> The auld black Deil a kintry claver;
> And what is sin, but saut to savour
>   Mankind's wersh luggies?
> While saunts, if ye'd believe the shaver,
>   Are kirk-gaun puggies.

[1] Mr. Hamish Hendry, in "The Beadle's Lament," in his volume "Burns from Heaven," Glasgow, 1897.

It is the function and the duty of every man to think and decide for himself as to life, and among other things to determine whether he counts Jesus reliable as an observer, if not as a guide. It is worth while, then, to remark that Jesus has no responsibility for this trivial treatment of evil—none. It is surprising to note how often, in the language of his day, picture-language not literal but intelligible to everybody, he refers to the worm and the fire, to darkness and gnashing of teeth. "How *can* you escape the damnation of hell?" he asked some people once, with a directness which, if we had the decency to be candid, we should call rather un-Christian in our sense, whoever used it. A man who deliberately put himself in the way of men who would undoubtedly crucify him—who did it with his eyes open—, cannot be saddled with responsibility for our flimsy views of right and wrong. The first step to win the respect of reasonable and sensible men and women for his religion must be to confess our disloyalty to him on this issue, and to attempt to draw his sharp distinction between right and wrong. This will not mean a return to a doctrine of hell which we have found inconsistent with his spirit and his teaching, but a frank and penitent recognition of the deepest contrast that the universe has to show. It is no compliment to him to suppose that he could have missed it.

V

More significant than the modern indifference to evil is the disbelief in good. Many thinkers have recognized evil as of tremendous power in human affairs; others have more or less equated them in influence, have found a sort of balance in the universe, and have allowed consequences to follow good where it was operative as surely as they follow evil. I have cited Virgil as witness to decline and degeneration in things physical, but one of his cardinal principles is summed up in his phrase *justissima tellus;* earth plays fair by you, gives back what you sow, and repays all the care and all the forethought you give her. The same idea is in a number of Jesus' parables; if bramble and rock are fatal to the grain, the good soil yields thirty, sixty, a hundred times the seed it receives.

To apply this to human life calls for a courage not common among moralists. To most men nothing is so disappointing as human nature. It is a proverb that politicians and statesmen let you down—not to put it more strongly; and they infest every part of life, not only the state but the church, the college, the town council, the vestry. It is a constant complaint that all commerce and business depend on dishonesty, though here Professor F. G. Peabody has brilliantly retorted by appealing to the Stock Exchange, the favourite illustration of those who disbelieve in truth as a real factor in the business world, and has pointed out that of its millions of contracts the vast majority are verbal and are kept. Preachers habitually emphasize the force of bad example, and are right, but they forget that Jesus at least believed good to be much more powerful.

It is quite plain to those who care to study him, that, while Jesus had no illusions about evil, while he recognized the eternal distinction between right and wrong as valid to the Judgment Day and beyond, he had a faith in good which is not exampled elsewhere. His belief in his power to influence men so raw and so slow as his disciples—his willingness to leave them so little matured as he did, to trust to them the whole of his work on earth—a venture hard to expect under similar circumstances from even the most like him of all his followers—his deliberate choice of the cross—all these speak, more plainly even than his parables and his general teaching, of his faith in good. God is behind it and in it, he saw, and there is nothing so fruitful at all. We have generally lost that confidence, and venture into His service again and again as a forlorn hope ("I shall one day fall by the hand of Saul," we say); and little is to be expected from work attempted in such a spirit. It is not justified, this diffidence of ours, as our own experience often proves, if we would only study it. Depression in sowing seed is a frame of mind recognized in the *Psalms* as not inconsistent with abundant harvest; the thing is to get the seed fairly into the ground. Jesus trusts both the seed and the soil, knowing Who made them both and made them for one another.

We have to recapture his faith in God, his conviction of God's nature and goodness, and his assurance that God triumphs in a world, which, after all, He appears to have designed for the carrying out of His own purposes. The Great White Throne is a vivid rendering of the faith of Jesus that Right is fundamentally different from Wrong and habitually and finally triumphs over Wrong, because God is with the Right. Certainly the story of the Christian Church, if we would take the trouble to know it and to understand it, should give us courage. Where has the Gospel failed, when men have taken it seriously, lived on it and secured that it was intelligibly presented to their fellow-men?

The grey world of our theology, or philosophy, or whatever we call it, is not the real world; it is not confirmed by good pagan thinkers; it is not in Jesus' picture of God. We pay the penalty inevitably whenever we try to live in a non-existent world. Greyness only belongs to a climate of cloud and fog; and the moral world is not grey, it is a region of colour, where the shadows are very black indeed, because the sunshine is very bright.

XIII

THE STUDY OF THE BIBLE

I

The story may be apocryphal, but it is told of a well-known poet, that his wife invaded his study one morning and set him to read "a portion of God's Word," that he obeyed, and that, when a little later his son came in and saw what he was reading, the poet looked up and said: "My boy, you should always read the Bible; there's nothing like it for your style."

There is a great deal in what the poet so unexpectedly said; but it turns on what we mean by style. For the moment let us be content to say that a race, in one way or another, produces a speech, which men of genius, if the race breed them, may develop into the most sensitive organ for expressing what is deepest and truest in human experience. By style we mean the instinct for using that organ to its full capacity, and style is acquired or perfected by familiarity with those who have it; it is a gift of association. The English speech is the slow-grown language of a race. Celt and Saxon and others have made and remade that race and that speech; but its character was given to race and to speech as much by the English Bible of 1611 and its predecessors, as by any other influence.

It is common knowledge that a committee never writes English; how King James' revisers escaped the common fate of committees and produced so great a monument of genuine English, is a theme well worthy of study. The first and most obvious solution of the problem is that the book was mainly the work of one man; but, even so, a group of men —two or three—will spoil the sense, the spirit, the cadences of the purest and strongest of writers. Tyndale, the author of the fabric on which the Jacobeans worked, was a sturdy, strong, if rather insular, character, with an inborn directness and grace of speech, and he had the great advantage of having no colleagues, none at least to whom he was bound to defer. To read the Gospels through in his version is to see how essentially he remains the English translator. Whatever the revisers of Geneva and of 1611 did, the body of the work was and is Tyndale's.[1] He had the good fortune to live and work at a time when men wrote by ear and instinct what they felt; and even in 1611 there was no journalism, no sham scientific jargon, and the flamboyant pedantries of Euphues and Holofernes were

[1] See Westcott (Aldis Wright), "History of English Bible," p. 158.

THE STUDY OF THE BIBLE

after all a better training. Pedantry is easier to get rid of than slovenliness.

Tyndale's mastery of English, plain and simple, but capable of strength and feeling in its purity, secured that the later versions should not be cast in another mould; and he and his successors set a standard for English for all time.

Selden complained that "the Bible is rather translated into English words than into English phrases. The Hebraisms are kept, and the phrase of that language is kept." Perhaps they were, here and there; but the structure of the Hebrew language, to which all faithful translators had to be loyal, was not so very alien to that of the English actually spoken by men, as William Wordsworth put it—not so alien that it was impossible or even difficult to transfer thoughts simply and naturally from the one to the other.[1] The simplicity of the original had a part in securing the simplicity of the rendering. But when even a translator like Chapman could so miss the directness of Homer as to make Troy "shed her towers for tears of overthrow," [2] the simplicity of the original is not a complete explanation. The dogma of inspiration forbade embroidery, and bound the translators to the strictest loyalty to the old and simple phrase that was consistent with the freedom of their own speech. Nor was the certainty of bitter

[1] This point did not escape Tyndale.
[2] See Matthew Arnold, "On Translating Homer," p. 29 (toward end of first essay).

controversy on every disputable passage without its effect. No doubt, the Biblical scholar can still recognize at a glance in a hundred places the Hebrew or the Greek behind the rendering, but the whole does not suggest a translation. It seems more native to us than the English prose of the period. In spite of the Hebraisms or Hellenisms that survived translation, in spite of Latinisms that stole in at a time when educated England Latinized deliberately and lapsed into Latin constructions by accident, the Bible of 1611 was in English; and its very Hebraisms and Hellenisms became English.

Even for those who read the Greek Testament freely enough, the Authorized Version is, in a way, more essentially the Word of God than the Greek text; it comes nearer home, it is God speaking in English more genuinely than men said He did in other tongues at Pentecost, in the language of the heart. Modern discovery has proved that "the language of the Holy Ghost," as scholars once called it, was just ordinary Greek, the speech in which men wrote letters to their wives and little boys to their fathers.[1] The language of our English Bible is for us instinct with more beauty than the Hellenistic Greek, it carries more associations; there are chords of sympathy within us, which that Greek tongue will not readily make vibrate, but which respond in an

[1] J. H. Moulton, "Prolegomena to Grammar of N.T. Greek," pp. 3, 5.

instant to the simpler and nobler speech of the generations that made our Reformation. It is in such a dialect that God and Nature speak to us—in words which want no dictionary or commentary, for the meaning of which we need no papyrus fragments to enlighten us. It is surely not fanciful to find a training in style in the study of such a language.

What the language of the English Bible can do for those who will read it with feeling, and surrender, we know from the books of John Bunyan and the speeches of John Bright. Ruskin, Carlyle, Newman, Wordsworth, all masters of style, had one view of the English Bible. In it Abraham Lincoln learnt the language in which he reached the hearts of men, he had "mastered it so that he became almost 'a man of one book.'" As Coleridge said, "intense study of the Bible will keep any writer from being vulgar in point of style."

Let us gather up our threads. "There's nothing like it for your style," said the poet. A race and a language grow up together, reacting on each other. If that language is yours, if you belong to that race, if you wish to speak to its heart, you must know both race and speech at their highest and best, and know them long. The Bible was done into English in the most formative generations of our history. It took long to perfect it, to assimilate every shade of meaning in the original and to give it again in English, but the task was achieved; and a version was made that has won and keeps the affection of Englishmen, and has done more than any other book—even if we count in Shakespeare—to mould our speech and to shape our national character.

II

Little consciousness is betrayed by the authors of the Gospels or by St. Paul [1] that their writing is inspired; Luke writes a preface, on the contrary, that suggests he felt himself like other men who write books, bound to use every faculty he had of study and research, of comparison and criticism. The great New Testament writers are like the Greeks animated by interest in their subject and the human feeling that other men must be interested in it too. Throughout the early ages of the Church the same conviction lived, and is witnessed to by the many translations made of the New Testament into the languages of the ancient world. For the early Church the Bible was an open book and its daily reading in the family was inculcated.[2] In the fourth and fifth centuries Jerome revised the Latin translation, not with complete approbation among contemporary churchmen for his presuming to meddle with

[1] Paul's words in 1 Cor. vii. 10, 12, 25, 40 are hard to construe into such a claim of inspiration as his readers have sometimes made on his behalf.

[2] Harnack, "Bible-Reading in the Early Church," p. 145, p. 55; Tertullian, "Ad Uxorem," ii. 6; Clement Alex., "Strom," vii. 7, 49.

a familiar text. And then followed a really strange development. With the fall of the Empire came new tongues, into some of which, Gothic, for example, the Bible was translated. But a nimbus grew up round Jerome's version, which neither he nor his contemporaries could have foreseen, and a dogma that Latin was after all the language of the Holy Ghost. The Vulgate of Jerome became canonized, and in the Middle Ages there was the bitterest opposition to the reading of the Bible in the native languages of the several countries. Roman Catholic writers deny this, but until they reply satisfactorily to the researches of scholarship, the denial is of no moment.

Thus Miss Deanesley in "The Lollard Bible," a work of remarkable learning, brings evidence to show that knowledge of the text of Scripture was in a layman a presumption of heresy; "the first and primary question is whether the suspected heretic has ever heard or learned the words of the German Gospels" (p. 62). The Waldensians "give all their zeal to lead many others astray with them; they teach even little girls the words of the gospels and epistles, so that they may be trained in error from their childhood" (p. 63). "For most people," she shrewdly concludes (p. 88), "assistance at a bookburning was a far more frequent source of education than the study of provincial synods," and there was plenty of opportunity for such education. "The value of an English Bible was not the foundation stone in John Wycliffe's theory for the reform of Church and State, but the practical measure to which his theories led him at the end of his life" (p. 225); and the essential novelty of the Wycliffite translations was that they were designed for publication, for reading in a wider public and a lower social class than royal dukes and other noble bibliophiles (p. 227). It was understood that the clergy did not want them to be read, and in Lollard trials witnesses often deposed that they had heard the accused reading in a book of the gospels in English, or some other biblical book, and therefore knew he was a heretic (p. 326). It followed that, when printing was established in England, the Scriptures in English were not printed for half a century.

It is arguable that educated England was more open in the sixteenth century to foreign ideas than in the nineteenth. First the Reformation and the Counter-Reformation, then Stuart wars, and finally the French Revolution all helped to secure our island against foreign influences. But one of the surprises that await the reader in the earlier century is the quick and keen transmission of ideas. Early in the reign of Henry VIII Cambridge scholars gathered quietly to an obscure inn in Plute's Lane—somewhere behind the present Bull Hotel or on the site of the new parts of King's College—to read the newcome works of Luther. Nor was Oxford im-

THE STUDY OF THE BIBLE

mune, though Cambridge is the University identified with the Reformation. As early as 1523 we find debate in a country house near Little Sodbury, in Gloucestershire, on the new ideas spreading from Germany upon religion. The tutor of the family, a young Gloucestershire man, himself educated at Oxford (but, regrettably, it seems not at Cambridge also, as was long ago believed) took up the cause of the new movement, and would argue with the guests of the house, "communing and disputing"—an admirable and Socratic way of learning—"with a certain learned man," writes Foxe,[1] "in whose company he happened to be, he drove him to that issue, that the learned man said, 'We were better be without God's laws than the Pope's.' Master Tyndale hearing that answered him, 'I defy the Pope and all his laws'; and said, 'If God spare my life, ere many years I will cause that a boy that driveth the plough shall know more of the Scripture than thou doest.'"

The promise is a famous one, and it was fulfilled within five years. For in 1525–1526, Tyndale put the first New Testament, rendered into English from the Greek, through the press—a translation made by himself from the third edition of Erasmus' Greek text—but at what cost! He had had to leave his native land for ever, to face, as he says, "poverty, exile, bitter absence from friends, hunger and thirst

[1] Edition of 1563, quoted by Demaus, "Tyndale" (1886), p. 72.

and cold, great dangers and innumerable other hard and sharp fightings." His book very soon, and himself at last (1536) were burnt; but enough copies escaped the flames to be multiplied anew in authentic and other editions, till at last he revised it himself and reissued it in 1534.

Tyndale's work drew upon him a great storm of denunciation. Tunstal, Bishop of London, preached against the book at Paul's Cross, and declared:

> That he found errors more or less
> Above three thousand in the translation.[1]

So wrote Roye, faithfully recording Tunstal's sermon, in a poem which displeased Tyndale; "it becometh not the Lord's servant to use railing rhymes." Three thousand blunders seems a large number. Sir Thomas More, who let himself go in invective against Tyndale more than once, was more moderate at this point; "above a thousand texts in it were wrong and falsely translated," it was "corrupted and changed from the good and wholesome doctrine of Christ to devilish heresies of his own."

Tyndale wrote a reply. "There is not so much as one *i* therein, if it lack a tittle over his head, but they have noted it, and number it unto the ignorant people for an heresy." He had foreseen that errors would occur. "Where they find faults, let them show it me, if they be nigh, or write to me if they

[1] Quoted by Demaus, "Tyndale," p. 150.

THE STUDY OF THE BIBLE

be far off; or write openly against it and improve it, and I promise them, if I shall perceive that their reasons conclude, I will confess mine ignorance openly." He goes further, and requests "that they put to their hand to amend it, remembering that so is their duty to do."

One of the main charges was that Tyndale used native English for the terms of Greek and Latin that had become technical. "You wrote," says an envoy of the English government to his chief, "that the answer which he made to the Chancellor was unclerkly done; and so seem all his works to eloquent men because he useth so rude and simple style. . . ." So men had said of the Old Latin, and of the Greek; so had Paul said of himself; so said the critics about Euripides [1] and Wordsworth in turn. "By this translation," wrote another, "shall we lose all these Christian words, penance, charity, confession, grace, priest, church, which he always calleth a congregation." This charge Sir Thomas More also took up,[2] but Tyndale was equal to a reply; certain of these terms were "the great juggling words wherewith, as St. Peter prophesied, the clergy made merchandise of the people." But he admitted that *seniors* for *priests* could be bettered, and substituted *elders*. Sir Thomas returned to the attack—he spent his later years on it voluminously—"This drowsy drudge

[1] Longinus, 40.
[2] His controversy with Tyndale, Demaus, "Tyndale," ch. ix.

hath drunken so deep in the devil's dregs, that, but if he wake and repent himself the sooner, he may hap ere aught long to fall into the mashing-fat, and turn himself into draff as the hogs of hell shall feed upon and fill their bellies thereof." More has a great name in English history, but neither that name nor his gifts in controversy can obscure the fact that the Greek *presbyteros* does mean *senior* or *elder* and does not mean *priest,* and never did till Cyprian's day; and why should the boy that driveth the plough not be told what the New Testament really said?

Other people even then saw more than this in Tyndale. "The man," wrote an envoy of Thomas Cromwell, "is of a greater knowledge than the King's Highness doth take him for, which well appeareth by his works." He had the instinct of the real scholar; his account of his view of translation anticipates Jowett's canons of interpretation. What did the author, *not* the commentator, mean to say? "Scripture," he wrote,[1] "hath but one sense, which is the literal sense. And that literal sense is the root and ground of all, and the anchor that never faileth, whereto if thou cleave thou canst never err or go out of the way. And if thou leave the literal sense, thou canst not but go out of the way. . . . Allegory proveth nothing, neither can do. For it is not the Scripture but an ensample or a similitude borrowed of the Scripture. . . . If I could not prove with an

[1] Demaus, "Tyndale," p. 198.

THE STUDY OF THE BIBLE

open text that which the allegory doth express, then were the allegory a thing to be jested at, and of no greater value than a tale of Robin Hood." If Luther pointed the way here, Tyndale had the solid sense to see that it was the right way, and all sound scholarship has followed in it ever since. "Authentic words be given, or none," was Wordsworth's judgment on doctored fragments of Simonides.

The soundness of Tyndale's scholarship was proved by the way it stood. Battle after battle was fought by Reformers and Papists, constantly on the ground of the text of Scripture; version after version was made, and the 1611 revisers were referred still to Tyndale, whom with others they used and whose wording like those others they kept. "It is impossible," wrote Professor B. F. Westcott,[1] "to read through a single chapter without gaining the assurance that Tyndale rendered the Greek text directly, while he still consulted the Vulgate, the Latin translation of Erasmus, and the German of Luther"; and later he adds that Tyndale used them "with the judgment of a scholar. His complete independence in this respect is the more remarkable from the profound influence which Luther exerted upon his writings generally." His prologue to Hebrews is cited as an illustration of this independence. It is noted—and this is surely an English trait—that he does not

[1] Westcott, "History of English Bible" (edited by W. Aldis Wright), pp. 132, 146.

allow so large a place to the reader's own subjective judgments as Luther. Fidelity to the text was his aim—always the scholar's aim: "I call God to record against the day we shall appear before our Lord Jesus Christ to give reckoning of our doings, that I never altered one syllable of God's word against my conscience." Sound learning, the use of the best helps available, independence, loyalty to his text and his author; to these add for a translator the language really used by men and the genius to make that language live and glow with the life and passion of the original; and little more can be asked.

"Our English tongue," wrote Thomas Fuller, a century later commingling blame and praise, "was not improved to that expressiveness whereat this day it is arrived." But the plain style has prevailed, and when Englishmen wish to be taken seriously, whether in prose or verse, they use essentially the language that Tyndale used; and William Wordsworth, in his preface to "Lyrical Ballads" in 1800, wrote the justification of that language.

Once more to sum up: It appears that Wycliffe and Tyndale had the same design—to put the Bible, and especially the New Testament, in the plainest and most intelligible English consistent with faithfulness to the original, into the hands of every man —of the "boy that driveth the plough"—to bring it effectively into national life, and to make it an integral element of the English character, understood and absorbed till it should transform English nature. And this they fairly achieved.

III

"Consider the great historical fact that, for three centuries, this book has been woven into the life of all that is best and noblest in English history; that it has become the national epic of Britain and is as familiar to noble and simple, from John o' Groat's House to Land's End, as Dante and Tasso once were to the Italians; that it is written in the noblest and purest English, and abounds in exquisite beauties of mere literary form; and finally, that it forbids the veriest hind who never left his village to be ignorant of the existence of other countries and other civilizations, and of a great past stretching back to the furthest limits of the oldest nations of the world."

So wrote T. H. Huxley, an independent witness, surely, if there was one (*Essays* iii, 397).

On 7 March 1528 John Pykas of Colchester was brought before Bishop Tunstal on a serious charge, and he confessed that "about two years last past he bought in Colchester, of a Lombard of London, a New Testament in English and paid for it four shillings, which New Testament he kept, and read it through many times." Nothing could keep Tyndale's book out of England, neither the government nor the price, for four shillings meant a good deal of money four centuries ago. The book was quietly hawked about; it was bought and read—"read through many times"—and fresh copies came, and then fresh versions; and what men learnt from it is, as Huxley says, woven into the very fabric of English life and history. How is a man to understand English life or English history if he has no knowledge of the book which Englishmen have read incomparably more intensely than any other literature at all?

Tyndale did other work with his pen beside translating the New Testament and some part of the Old; and in one of his other books we read: "Though every man's body and goods be under the king, do he right or wrong, yet is the authority of God's Word free and above the king; so the worst in the realm may tell the king, if he do him wrong, that he doth naught." A century later Charles I. succeeded to the throne of a nation which had steadily read Tyndale's Testament, the Genevan and the others, for a hundred years, and he found a people transformed from the subjects of Henry VIII. Tyndale did not stop there. "If my neighbour need and I give him not, neither depart [*i.e.* divide, as in the marriage formula] liberally with him of that which I have, then withhold I from him unrighteously that which is his own. . . . In those goods which are gotten most

THE STUDY OF THE BIBLE 259

truly and justly are men much beguiled. For they suppose they do no man wrong in keeping them." It has a surprisingly modern sound, this sentiment—surprising at least for those who suppose that social righteousness was an idea first hatched in the later nineteenth century and outside the churches.

It was at Worms that Tyndale made his translation of the New Testament. The next of the three great English versions was made at Geneva by the friends of John Knox—a name that recalls a great deal of Scottish history, the threads of which are all interwoven with the Bible. As for England, the Puritan emigrations; the long and painful battles at home for freedom, for the emancipation of the negro, for the Factory Acts; the steady inculcation of duty; the teaching of all the philosophy Englishmen or perhaps Scots really have, the fostering of independence—everything of moment in our life and history—is linked with the study of this book. Other lands have their histories as well as England and Scotland; what of Imperial Rome, of Spain and Germany, of France and Russia, ancient and modern? Is it not true that the Bible and the religion connected with it have been at or near the heart of all the great movements of civilized men? Not perhaps of the movements that make noise for a while and after that have a mere antiquarian interest, but the real movements—Constantine, the Crusades, the Reformation, the planting of America, and even modern democracy, Transatlantic and Tolstoian. In one way or another, appealing or rejected, the Bible is relevant to them all. The formative men, as we have seen, have again and again been under its influence, consciously or unconsciously. If our study of History is to be more than formal or superficial we have to reckon with the power exerted by the Bible.

Once again let us sum up what we have reached. The original writers of the Bible were men speaking to men of what they deemed to be supremely relevant; and so it proved. After three centuries Jerome felt it urgent for the Latin-speaking world to have their exact word and thought, as closely rendered as scholarship and old associations would allow. After other centuries Wycliffe had Jerome's version done into English, or did it himself, because it was to give the motive and the assurance for a better national life. Later again Erasmus devoted himself in Cambridge to editing as correct a Greek text of the New Testament as the known manuscripts and the existing knowledge of their relations with one another permitted. That text Luther did into German, and Tyndale into English with every care, in the same conviction that the books bore upon life as no others did. The literary work of both men went far to shape the history of German and of English literature, and the social and political effects of their translations justified their belief that the two Testaments were relevant to the life of their time and every time.

A century of translators, and four centuries of readers have woven the Bible into national life, national speech and national literature. If style is to be achieved by models, here is the most essentially native book in our tongue, more English (in spite of its Hebrew and Greek originals) than any other English book, more widely accepted than any other, and more intimately related in word and history to the genius of our people. To know intensely the genius of one's people, their mind, their deepest hopes and aspirations, their memories, associations and intimacies, the things that mean nothing to strangers and everything to them—some such training will be necessary for the man who is to speak to his people in a language that will reach and stir their hearts. Other elements have indeed gone to the making of the English people, but that does not alter the fact that the Bible is something very like

The master-light of all our seeing.

Men quote it relevantly and irrelevantly; its phrases pervade our speech; its cadences and rhythms haunt our writers and speakers; and with serious thinkers of our race it is common knowledge that here they touch what is most fundamental in all life.

IV

"Style," said the finest of ancient critics, "is the echo of a great nature" ("γψος μεγαλοφροσύνης ἀπήχημα). Whether we render the word of Longinus a great nature, or a great soul, or a great mind, the adjective is constant, and the translators mean the same thing. Mind, soul, nature—the fundamental being of the man, his very essence must have greatness, if he is to manage that greatest of achievements—speech that reaches the heart of man and lives there for ever. "We have to do with an endowment rather an acquirement," says Longinus; it is "a thing given" rather than one "gained"; but all the same the gift has to be developed, we must "nurture our souls, as far as is possible, to all that is great (πρὸς τὰ μεγέθη), and make them, as it were, pregnant with noble inspiration. . . . It is not possible for men whose thoughts are mean and slavish, and whose lives embody such thoughts, to put forth anything that is wonderful or worthy of immortality. It is from the lips of men of high spirit that the great accents fall." Longinus illustrates his thesis with a saying of Alexander, but a gap in the manuscript cuts it away. Later on, where the manuscript serves us again, he is quoting Homer to show how greatly men may conceive of gods, and then somewhat to the surprise of those who know how little apt Greeks were to look outside their own national literature, he adds: "Thus too the lawgiver of the

Jews, no ordinary man, worthily conceived and worthily expressed the power of the Godhead, when at the very beginning of his laws he wrote, 'God said'—what? 'Let there be light and there was light; let there be earth and there was earth.'"[1]

So to achieve style we need the dower of a great soul, and we have to give it a great training. We must be able "to choose," as Longinus goes on to say, "the most vital things," and to "make them form as it were one body."[2] The English words have lost their value and lustre; a *corpus juris,* a *corpus inscriptionum,* and their English equivalents suggest death, the Greek word suggests life. What are, in anything we have to understand and then perhaps to describe, the essential things, the things that make it what it is and without which it would not be that at all? It is a task of spiritual diagnosis. Can you recapture these, and then—the word will come back to the English pen, though it is wrong—*fuse* them? No, not *fuse* them, but so bring them together that together they form a living whole. A tragedy, said Aristotle long before,[3] must be "a whole of some magnitude, and a whole is something that has beginning, middle, and end; it is the same for the beautiful and for the living creature." He uses the comparison of the living animal and not idly. Life, the

[1] Longinus, 9.
[2] Longinus, 10.
[3] Aristotle, "Poetics," 7, p. 1450 *b.*

organic relation of whole and part, the essential, the vital—a man of genius is needed to know these and

Out of three sounds to make, not a fourth sound, but a star.

Given genius, or some gift that might develop into it, what is to be its training? How is one to train the instinct for what Longinus calls τὰ καιριώτατα —the most essential? Here Plato, as always, comes to our help. "The unexamined life is unlivable for a human being," he says in a sentence that can hardly be quoted too often; and elsewhere he adds that man is to practice "the contemplation, the study of all time and all existence." Postponing "all existence" for a moment, we are called on to study all human experience, a large task; we are to be heirs of all the ages and to enter effectively on our inheritance. Nothing human is to be alien to us, but we have to know exactly what is vital and essential in it. I string together phrases from the Classics, because I want to relate our particular subject to literature, thought and experience in general; and after all it is only carrying out Plato's injunction.

The great danger of modern education is the groove. Even the Universities now conceive it part of their function to be technical schools in a practical age, and a man may graduate Master of Arts (so forgetful are we of the meaning of words and the ideals they are meant to carry) on a knowledge of one art only or one science, if a knowledge of bolts and rivets and cranks is rightly to be called either science or art. Can a man be called educated who has never intellectually got outside the insular and the contemporary? Can he be called a man at all? It is not so that men are made. At the dawn of history, the poet gives us a man who "saw the cities of many men and learnt their mind." It was this gift of travel in the things of the mind that made Greece, this faculty for human experience, getting inside the minds of many men, very alien men, strange in habit, tradition and outlook. When Greece grew too great to learn any more from the barbarian her decline began. Her rejuvenator, Alexander the Great, was one of those great minds everywhere at home and everywhere alive to human greatness, everywhere capable of understanding it and enjoying it. Is it possible that we Anglo-Saxons, who are not usually considered by impartial observers to have all the gifts and graces of the Greek (to say nothing of the Italian and some other races not ungifted), that we, of all people, can be sufficient to ourselves? Was Heine's *ächtbrittische Beschränktheit* really meant for praise? Does it really help us?

Here then is a whole literature ready to our hand very foreign indeed, and yet not foreign but familiar, woven into our own race and speech as we have seen, without which our own stock is not intelligible, a literature which will reveal to us our own people and the foreigner. In speech and thought, in lanworld are amazingly intelligible without commentaries at all. Callimachus may need the commentator, and be worthless when explained. How much has been written of the *Odyssey* to elucidate it for scholars—and a child of five may be at home in it for ever! Real people always understand real books, and real books only need real people; and not all commentators are supremely real, or they might be doing something more original. Is there not something to be said for the training of Mary Lamb, tumbled, as her brother said, into a room full of good literature? Is there not something of this in the practice of encouraging children to begin the regular habit of Bible-reading, if only for education? Let them really read it, and they will understand fast enough what is meant for them; and what is harder, or what older (and duller) people call unsuitable, they will pass over, and it will not hurt them. The effort to penetrate the foreign medium—puzzling out the allusions to foreign ways that perplex, comparing, reflecting—is it not essentially Odysseus again "seeing the cities of many men and learning their mind"? And, when one reflects of how many English generations they will be repeating the experience, it will not seem improbable that they will end with more understanding of their own people.

But after all, as we have seen, it is τὰ καιριώτατα, the essential and vital things, that matter. The worst of current literature is that it is unsorted;

we read, like the undergraduate Wordsworth, "lazily in trivial books" and forget them very properly, but our time may be gone. This is where the Classics of the races count; they have not lived for nothing. In this busy and careless world, where we "scrap" everything we can, and as soon as we can, some books refuse to be "scrapped," they go living on. When a book can maintain itself for a century, there is something in it, when for many centuries, there is a great deal in it; and when it laughs at oceans and barriers of race and speech as well as at time, we may be sure it is relevant to us; when we feel, as Montaigne did about Plutarch, that "we cannot do without him," what quality does that imply? and when myriads of men and women of different races and cultures, in widely remote lands and ages, say of the Bible in all sorts of translations that they "cannot do without it," what does that mean? Does it not suggest that here they find what they know to be real in the deepest sense? Boswell and Wordsworth are very dear to Englishmen, but somehow foreigners miss them. Isaiah and Luke, Paul and Jeremiah, have a way of finding their audience; much of the Psalms may be foreign, but how much is essentially human? If Longinus calls Moses "no ordinary man," what of the greater figures in that literature? The great soul is implied in the wholesale capture of men and generations—the great soul with the great experience behind it and the great thoughts welling up within it, however simple the language. Perhaps the last thing Paul thought of was style, yet a well-known German scholar tells us that he catches again in certain chapters of the epistles to the Romans and Corinthians just that great note which Greek literature had once had, but had lost for centuries.[1] If it were only convention, is it not well to know and understand the conventions of the people one meets—in books or streets? But if it is a question of knowing what the generations have counted vital, should we not train ourselves, and teach our children, to be pleased with the best? Trivial tastes, pleasure in the commonplace, are no training for the great soul. It is customary with people who do not know Latin to suppose that education means *educing* something in a child; the more real meaning is to bring a child out—out of what, or into what? Surely into the real world, out of half-worlds and barren regions, into the best and the eternal.

If education is to make a man free of the world, to open to him the doors that lead to the real things, the last great question is, Whose world is it? Wordsworth in the "Ode on Intimations of Immortality" describes how the interests of life gather thick about the growing boy, and close his eyes to the heaven that lies about us in our infancy, and crowd out that faculty of wonder, which, Plato said,

[1] Norden, in his "Kunstprosa," writing of Paul.

is the mother of philosophy. Yes, the interests and occupations of life overbear us, and "lay waste our powers," and we miss τὰ καιριώτατα. But on some men comes a sense of God, when and how, no man can predict. The rich man will rebuild his barns, and settle down to a life of rest and enjoyment; and there comes a tap on the shoulder; he wheels round and is face to face with—God!

> There's a sunset touch
> A fancy from a flower-bell, some one's death,
> A chorus-ending from Euripides,—
> And that's enough for fifty hopes and fears
> As old and new at once as nature's self.[1]

One cannot live on the surface for ever, for ever haunt the circumference; when we begin to get below the surface a little, to dream of depths and to think out a centre—where are we? We are in the company of psalmist and prophet, apostle and philosopher, pressing on to God. It must be God. But here we may lose ourselves in a dreamy mysticism, and, in contemplation of the abstract, drift at last with empty hands to nothing. No, that is to lose the value of human experience, tears and love and laughter, pain and friendship. And that is where the Bible and its writers, and its centuries of readers, help us; for with them God is not abstract. They feel Him in the words of Christ; they touch Him in the person of Christ; not abstract at all, He

[1] Browning, "Bishop Blougram's Apology."

is intelligible and lovable in those pages—real. How are we to live in a real world at all, if the record of His discovery, of His revelation, is a sealed book to us, if His Incarnation is an idle word for us, if the surface of things is all, and the end a question mark?

THE END